Funny helpful tips:

Your essence is not defined by external accolades, but by the depth of your character and integrity.

Set clear boundaries; they protect your energy and define your personal space.

Exploit Expatriate Tax Breaks for Big Savings : Maximize Your Tax Savings as an Expat: Proven Strategies to Benefit from Overseas Tax Breaks

Life advices:

Limit refined carbohydrates; they can lead to energy crashes and weight gain.

Your dreams are the wings that propel you forward; nurture them with dedication and belief.

Introduction

This guide is a comprehensive resource designed to help Americans living overseas navigate the complex world of US taxation. It covers a wide range of topics, providing valuable insights and guidance to ensure expatriates remain compliant with US tax laws and maximize available benefits.

Before delving into the intricacies of expat taxation, the guide emphasizes the importance of taking essential steps before moving abroad. These steps include maintaining a US bank account, a US mailing address, and a US phone number. It also advises readers to evaluate their state tax obligations and consider using a VPN service to protect their online privacy.

The guide goes on to explain why Americans living abroad should care about US tax obligations. It debunks common myths and misconceptions surrounding taxation for expatriates, providing clarity on who must file US tax returns and the potential penalties for non-compliance.

One of the central components of the guide is the discussion of tax benefits for expats. It explores in detail the Foreign Earned Income Exclusion (FEIE), helping readers understand how it works, how to qualify, and its limitations. The guide also covers the Foreign Housing Exclusion or Deduction and the Foreign Tax Credit, providing practical examples to illustrate their application.

Tax treaty benefits, including income tax treaties, are explained to give readers insights into how they can further optimize their tax situation when living abroad.

Reporting foreign assets and bank accounts is a crucial aspect of expat taxation, and the guide discusses the Foreign Bank Account Report (FBAR) and Form 8938. It provides clarity on who needs to file these reports and the requirements for compliance.

US state tax considerations for expatriates, including strategies to minimize state tax liabilities, are also covered, ensuring that readers are well-informed about their obligations and potential savings opportunities.

The guide addresses various scenarios, such as expats who are married to US citizens, have children, or are legally married in another country. It explains how these situations can impact tax obligations and credits for dependents.

Additionally, it delves into investment and retirement planning, addressing topics like US retirement plans, foreign social security, and the taxation of retirement distributions.

For those involved in real estate, cryptocurrencies, or running businesses abroad, the guide provides insights into the tax implications and strategies for optimizing their financial situation.

Moreover, it covers essential aspects like filing back taxes and resolving non-compliance, offering options such as the IRS Streamlined Compliance Procedure.

The guide also includes a section on renouncing US citizenship, discussing the tax and other implications, costs, and the renunciation process.

Finally, it offers practical advice on how to file an expat tax return, including do-it-yourself options, US-based CPAs, and expat tax experts, along with important tax due dates and recordkeeping requirements.

In summary, this book is a comprehensive and invaluable resource for expatriates, providing guidance on various aspects of US taxation and compliance to help them make informed financial decisions while living abroad.

Contents

Chapter 1: Steps To Take Before Moving Abroad 1

    1.   Keep A US Bank Account (Or Two) 2

    2.   Maintain A United States Mailing Address 3

    3.   Keep A US Phone Number 4

    4.   Evaluate Your State 4

    5.   Sign Up For A VPN Service 5

    6.   Talk To A Tax Accountant Experienced With Expat Taxes 6

Chapter 2: Why You Should Care About US Tax WhenLiving Abroad 6

    Common Myths Expats Believe About Taxation 6

    Who Must File US Tax Returns? 8

    Penalties And Fines For Non-Compliance 10

    Penalties For Business Owners 11

    Green Card Holders 11

    Other People Who Meet The Substantial Presence Test 12

    Tax Benefits For Expats 13

Chapter 3: The Foreign Earned Income Exclusion 13

    What Is The Foreign Earned Income Exclusion And How DoesIt Work? 14

    Prorating The FEIE 14

    How To Qualify For The Foreign Earned Income Exclusion 15

    Foreign Earned Income 15

    Tax Home In A Foreign Country 16

    Physical Presence Test Vs. Bona Fide Residence In A ForeignCountry 16

    Physical Presence Test 17

    Bona Fide Residence Test.. 18

IRS Waiver Of Time Requirement Due To COVID 20

How To Use The Foreign Earned Income Exclusion (WithExample) 20

Common Mistakes When Claiming The FEIE 21

Chapter 4: The Foreign Housing Exclusion Or Deduction 24

What Is The Foreign Housing Exclusion Or Deduction And HowDoes It Work? 24

Exclusion Or Deduction? 25

Foreign Housing Exclusion Limits 25

High-Cost Locations 26

Eligible Housing Expenses 26

How To Use The Foreign Housing Exclusion Or Deduction(With Example) 27

Chapter 5: The Foreign Tax Credit 28

Can I Claim The Foreign Tax Credit? 28

Foreign Tax Credit Carryovers And Carrybacks 31

How To Use The Foreign Tax Credit (With Example) 31

Should Expats Use The Foreign Tax Credit Or The ForeignEarned Income
Exclusion? 32

Chapter 6: Tax Treaty Benefits 34

Income Tax Treaties 34

Taxation Of Social Security And Pensions 35

Saving Clause 35

Income Re-Sourcing 36

Social Security Totalization Agreements 36

Chapter 7: Reporting Foreign Assets And Bank Accounts 38

FBAR For Foreign Financial Accounts 38

Who Needs To File An FBAR? 39

Accounts With A Foreign Spouse 40

FBAR For Business Owners 41

How To File An FBAR (Foreign Bank Account Report) 41

If You Haven't Filed Even Though You Met The Threshold 42

Form 8938 For Other Specified Foreign Financial Assets 42

Who Needs To File Form 8938? 43

Foreign Assets That Don't Need To Be Reported 45

Chapter 8: US State Tax Considerations For Expats 46

Easy Vs. Difficult States For Expats 46

Move States To Save Tax 47

Chapter 9: Married & Children Abroad 49

Married To A US Person 49

US Person Married To A Non-Resident Alien 50

Head Of Household With An NRA Spouse And Dependents 52

Legally Married In Another Country 53

Credits For Children And Dependents 54

Chapter 10: Investing And Retirement Planning WhenAbroad 56

US Retirement Plans 56

More Retirement Planning Options For Business Owners 61

Foreign Social Security 67

Taxation Of Retirement Distributions 68

The Risk Of Foreign Investments, Life Insurances, AndPension Plans To Be Taxed
As PFIC 69

Real Estate In The US And Abroad 70

Taxation Of Cryptocurrencies 73

Chapter 11: Filing Back Taxes And Other Non-ComplianceResolution 75

Penalties And Other Repercussions Of Not Filing 75

Options For Catching Up On Back Taxes 77

IRS Streamlined Compliance Procedure 77

Chapter 12: Tax For US Business Owners Abroad 78

Most Common Mistakes When Incorporating 79

Having A US LLC Or S Corporation While Living Abroad 80

Disadvantages Of C Corporations 84

Having A Foreign Business 84

FBAR For Business Owners 92

Offshore Banking 92

Amazon Sellers And Other E-Commerce Entrepreneurs 95

Chapter 13: Self-Employed Abroad 96

Taxes For Self-Employed Individuals Abroad 96

Reporting Self-Employment Income Earned Abroad 97

Quarterly Estimated Payments 98

How To Optimize Self-Employment Tax On Foreign Income 99

Chapter 14: Tax Considerations For Digital Nomads 100

Tax Home For Claiming The Foreign Earned Income Exclusion 100

State Tax 101

Remote Workers, Freelancers, And Entrepreneurs 101

Chapter 15: Renouncing Citizenship 103

Tax And Other Implications Of Citizenship Renunciation 103

Cost Of Renouncing 104

Covered Expats And Exit Taxes 105

Tax Planning Prior To Renouncing 106

Social Security And Retirement Payments After Renouncing 107

Renunciation Process 107

Chapter 16: Filing Your Expat Tax Return 110

DIY Software 110

US-Based CPA 110

Expat Tax Experts..111

How To Choose An Accountant..111

Chapter 17: Tax Due Dates And Recordkeeping 113

Expat Tax Calendar 113

Tax And Other Records You Should Keep 115

Chapter 1: Steps To Take Before Moving Abroad

Before explaining the tax benefits for expats in detail, let's talk about what you can do before your move to make tax season, and life in general, easier.

Moving to a foreign country is complicated. It's difficult to know where to start and what to focus on. And, unfortunately, good advice on how to prepare for a move is difficult to find, especially when it comes to complex topics like banking and tax. Public forums and Facebook groups are full of misleading, contradictory, and sometimes plain wrong information.

After helping over 3,000 expats and living abroad for 15 years ourselves, we have learned firsthand how to make the transition abroad as easy as possible.

In this chapter, we address the six things that expats can, and should, do before they leave the United States.

1. Keep A US Bank Account (Or Two)

You might think you won't have much use for a US bank account when living abroad. We suggest keeping at least two US accounts open. Ideally, they should be at two different banks.

Dealing with the IRS is perhaps the most important reason for maintaining a US bank account. People have a difficult time paying the IRS and receiving refunds if they don't have a US bank account. The IRS does not deposit into foreign accounts. Mailing checks to foreign addresses is often not feasible, and even if you get a paper check, it can be difficult to deposit abroad. The COVID stimulus payments also highlighted how useful a bank account in the US is.

In addition, a US bank account is convenient. Banking in the United States is generally easy. The US system makes it simple to send money abroad and most American banks offer user-friendly phone apps and credit card perks. (As a quick tip, make sure to download these banking apps while in the United States. These apps are often not available to download outside of the US). Additionally, access to English speaking staff at US banks makes interactions simple and problems easier to solve. Banking in an unknown or second language can quickly become a stressful and complicated endeavor.

Consider how often you will need funds in the US for purchases, bills, or payments. International transaction and wire fees can be costly, and wires may take several days to clear. If you have bills, family, or business in the US that you would like to send money to or receive money from, a US bank account is the easiest and most affordable way to do it.

Furthermore, the American banking system has an excellent international reputation. When it comes to business, US banks are among the most well regarded and trusted. This may not be an issue for those who are moving to countries with other well-regarded banking systems. However, individuals relocating to countries that frequently make the OECD's grey or blacklists have more cause for concern.

Since the enactment of the Foreign Account Tax Compliance Act (FATCA) and the Common Reporting Standard (CRS), many banks in other countries are hesitant to open accounts for Americans. Likewise, US banks are not especially open to Americans who live overseas either. For banks, US expatriates mean extra reporting requirements and more risk. Not only is it more difficult to open bank accounts abroad now, but some banks will even close existing accounts owned by US taxpayers who live overseas.

For many expats, these changes have made banking and life abroad exceptionally difficult. Many partially attribute the increase in the US citizenship renunciations to the implementation of FATCA and CRS.

Consider maintaining checking and savings accounts in at least two different US banks. Within the bureaucracy and regulations of banking, there are a variety of ways that banks can make your life difficult. By having a backup US account, expats can have peace of mind knowing that they have options. And, with many low fee or no-fee accounts, it's hard to see a disadvantage.

If you do not have a second bank account, open one before leaving the United States. In some cases, you may need to mail in paperwork or visit a bank branch to open the account or prove your identity. If possible, look for an account and card without foreign transaction fees and that reimburses ATM fees such as Charles Schwab.

Keep in mind what home and mailing address you will use for the bank. Generally, banks will want a domestic US address. This brings me to the next recommendation.

2. Maintain A United States Mailing Address

Even when living abroad you need a US mailing address for US banking and a variety of other reasons, such as renewing a US driver's license or voting in local elections.

Of course, you could use a relative's or friend's address, but this can be a hassle for them if you receive a lot of mail. To ensure that you do not miss anything important, they may have to open some mail for you. This means you would need to be very comfortable with them seeing confidential information, such as banking documents. Virtual mail services can be used to eliminate this issue.

These services will scan the outside of your mail, and you can choose to have it shredded, forwarded to you, or opened and scanned to you. The recipient can then decide whether they would like the opened mail to be shredded or forwarded.

These companies are usually significantly quicker than government mailing services. Not all countries have strong mailing systems. In some countries, international mailing times through government systems can take months.

As an example, a mail forwarding service in Panama can generally deliver a package from the US to Panama in a week. But, if mailed from the States with USPS and Panama's national mailing system, expect to wait about 6 to 8 months before the Panamanian mail system delivers it or notifies you that it is ready for pickup. There's a chance it may never even get delivered. This can happen in Europe too. Before moving, speak with expats in that country or check online forums to see how mailing works and what virtual mail companies are recommended.

We generally do not recommend using a PO box as they can create some complications. Banks and other entities may not accept PO boxes as an official address and some companies (like FedEx and DHL) won't ship to them.

Finally, check the tax laws of the state that the address is in. The wrong choice could trigger state taxes--even while you're living in another country. (More about state taxes in Chapter 8).

3. Keep A US Phone Number

Most expats are glad to ditch their expensive US phone bills, but they should keep their US phone number. It can be very convenient.

For example, not all websites allow space for international dialing codes and some will not send texts to international numbers. This can become a big issue if you need to receive a code to your phone for two-factor authentications or when you forget a password. Banks in particular often rely on this method to authenticate a login.

Another reason some expats keep their US phone number is to establish or maintain a US presence for their business and make it easier for US clients to call them. This can be especially important for expat business owners who service mainly American clients.

Likewise, a US phone number makes it easy to stay connected if you have US friends or family who aren't tech-savvy enough for WhatsApp, Facetime, WeChat, KakaoTalk, or other messaging services.

So how do you keep a US phone number without the hefty bill? Free or affordable options include Google Voice, Google Project Fi, Magic Jack, or a paid Skype account. There are also more complex setups for expats that need landlines, but you will need to be tech-savvy and willing to invest some time and money. As a quick tip, you can call US toll free numbers (usually +1 800, 888, 877, or 866) from Skype for free. Sometimes foreign phone plans that offer US minutes don't include US toll-free numbers.

4. Evaluate Your State

More than a few expats have had the unpleasant surprise of receiving notice from a US state that they owe state taxes.

Often, expats assume that once they leave the United States, they are free from state taxes. In reality, this is often incorrect. Some US states do levy taxes to Americans living abroad. These states assume that you will come back and therefore should remain a tax resident for the entire time spent abroad. Expats who are residents of such states need to show that they have no intention of ever returning to that state.

To avoid owing state income tax while abroad, consider leaving the state and cutting ties before leaving the country. This means changing your address, voter registration, local utility bills, leases, etc. Depending on the state, there may be a formal process to cancel residency.

The best states for expats are ones that do not have an individual income tax or that will stop considering you a resident if you have been gone for a certain amount of time. In Chapter 8, we go into more detail about how states handle expat taxation and how to minimize state taxes while living abroad.

5. Sign Up For A VPN Service

This one is optional but can certainly be useful. Consider signing up for a VPN service to protect your internet activity for security and to make it appear as if you are in another country.

VPNs help protect the user's private information and make it more difficult for online activity to be traced. This is essential for anyone concerned about privacy. Public Wi-Fi in places like airports, coffee shops, restaurants, or libraries can put users at risk. These types of places rarely have secure Wi-Fi, which means info that is typed while on the network (like usernames and passwords) can be stolen. But with a VPN, the user's info is encrypted and protected.

In addition, a VPN can give access to US-only services even from other countries. This is especially important when it comes to banking. A login from abroad might trigger your bank to flag or lock your account (which can often require calling their customer service hotline, which is a whole new problem when abroad. This is another good reason to keep a US phone number). Logging in with a VPN first reduces the chances of this happening.

One particular banking service that usually requires a VPN connection is mobile check deposit. When outside of the United States, this service typically isn't available. But by using a US IP address with a VPN, you can often circumvent this and still deposit US checks via your bank's mobile app. Even if you do not expect to receive any US checks while living abroad, you might be surprised at how often it comes up.

A similar situation can occur on some US government websites. When logging in from a foreign IP address, they may block your access. Alternately, many countries censor or block US social media and messaging sites. The right VPN can again remedy both of these issues.

One last perk, with a VPN, expats can access Netflix's American programs, other TV streaming services like HBO, and live sports.

Make sure the VPN company you use is reputable as some sell or keep records of user data. In addition, make sure that it will help you access the sites most important to you and is compatible with whichever computer or phone system you use. If you have a family, it's also worth checking how many devices can connect at once.

6. Talk To A Tax Accountant Experienced With Expat Taxes

Maybe so far you have been doing your taxes yourself, or you have a great US-based tax accountant. However, specific filing requirements, tax regulations, and IRS forms for American taxpayers abroad are different. It's easy to overlook potential tax savings or file forms incorrectly when not familiar with the Foreign Earned Income Exclusion, Housing Exclusion/Deduction, Foreign Tax Credit, tax treaties, and more. Talk to an international tax expert so you don't lose out on expat tax benefits. An experienced CPA can explain the tax impact for your specific situation and also advise you on moving to a different state before moving abroad.

Chapter 2: Why You Should Care About US Tax When Living Abroad

Many Americans think that they don't have to deal with US taxes when they move abroad. Unfortunately, this couldn't be further from the truth. As a US citizen or Green Card holder, you have to file a US expat tax return, each and every year. This is true even when living abroad and even if you don't owe any tax. US taxes for an American abroad can be overwhelming and confusing. Even worse, if you fail to file or make a mistake, it can result in significant penalties or even legal repercussions.

However, when prepared and filed correctly, there are huge benefits designed specifically for US expats.

This chapter explains taxation for US persons abroad. It includes common myths, filing thresholds, penalties, and tax benefits for Americans abroad.

Common Myths Expats Believe About Taxation

The US federal tax code is over 6,000 pages long as of 2022. That's without considering the statutory code, regulations and revenue rulings, and case law. It is no surprise that many misconceptions exist. Unfortunately, expats are not immune to them. An abundance of inaccurate information circulates on expat forums, groups, and blogs. Only a few accountants specialize in the taxation of US taxpayers abroad, so most US-based accountants don't know the specifics, either. Still, ignorance of the law is not an excuse for failing to file.

As accountants, here are five myths that we hear the most frequently:

Myth 1: Expats Don't Need To File US Taxes Because...

This has a few variations. Some say that expats do not need to file because foreign income is not taxed. Others believe that they can exclude foreign income of less than $100,000 and therefore they don't need to file.

These statements are all incorrect. US citizens, residents, and Green Card holders must file taxes every year, if they meet the filing thresholds (more on these in a minute), regardless of where they live or where their income comes from. While you may be able to exclude income, the process is nuanced. We explain how the Foreign Earned Income Exclusion works and how to use it in Chapter 3.

Expats who haven't filed taxes for multiple years because of this myth should skip straight to Chapter 11 and set up a consultation with an accountant specializing in expat tax to catch up on their back taxes. The penalties for failure to file, failure to pay, accumulated interest, underpayment penalty, and potential criminal penalties can be significant.

Myth 2: If You Haven't Filed Or Forgot To File You Are Facing Huge Fines No Matter What

This is not necessarily true. US persons may be able to get back into compliance without incurring any fines or penalties.

The IRS offers various amnesty programs for delinquent taxpayers. The Streamlined Filing Compliance Program is the most popular and often most applicable. We explain this program and other options in detail in Chapter 11.

If you are behind on your taxes it is crucial that you contact an expert tax accountant or attorney as soon as possible. Without proper and timely action, the repercussions of back taxes can be serious.

Myth 3: When I Renounce My US Citizenship, I Get Rid Of All US Tax Obligations

Unfortunately, it's not that easy. After you renounce, you must file a dual status tax return. This is a non-resident tax return with a resident dual status statement attached to it. Plus, during the renunciation process, you must file an additional exit tax return, even if you did not exceed thresholds for paying the exit tax. You could also potentially incur a hefty exit tax. (More on this in Chapter 15).

Even when you are no longer a US citizen, you must pay tax on some activities inside the United States. This includes rental income and selling real estate, dividends, and distributions from US-sourced securities or pensions. If you, as a non-US person, give a gift to a US person, such as a family member, the US person may need to report any gift above $100,000, however, it will not be taxed.

The tax implications of renouncing citizenship and how to minimize those taxes are explained in Chapter 15.

Myth 4: If I Set Up An Offshore Company, I Won't Pay Any Taxes

Owning an offshore company does not mean that you will not pay taxes. In some cases, owning an offshore company can result in a higher tax burden. This is true even when the offshore company is based in a zero-tax jurisdiction.

Offshore companies are part of a larger strategy that includes tax optimization. How an offshore company is taxed depends on several factors including what the company does, what assets it holds, and the structure it is a part of.

Myth 5: I Don't Need To Report My Foreign Bank Account Because I Have Less Than $10,000 In The Account

Misunderstanding the FBAR can have serious repercussions. The civil penalty for willful failure to report foreign bank accounts is either $129,210 or 50% of the total balance of the foreign accounts, whichever is higher. Even if you didn't know that you had to report those accounts, the penalty can be up to $12,921 per year. That means if you failed to report your foreign accounts several years in a row, you have to file an FBAR for each year and could potentially be liable for up to $12,921 in penalties for each of those years.

US citizens must report all foreign financial accounts if the combined value of the accounts exceeds $10,000 at any one time in the year.

For example, an expat has one foreign bank account with a highest balance of $5,000 on April 1 and a second foreign bank account with a highest balance of $6,000 on April 1. They need to file the Foreign Bank Account Report (FBAR) because the combined balance of their accounts at one time ($5,000+$6,000) totals $11,000 which puts them over the $10,000 FBAR filing threshold.

Chapter 7 explains in detail who must report foreign accounts and how to do it.

Who Must File US Tax Returns?

Taxation existed in Egypt as early as 3000–2800 BC. Since then, taxes have been a part of most societies. However, the US has a somewhat unusual method of taxation.

In the United States, taxes are applied based on citizenship, regardless of where the individual lives or earns income. The US is one of only two countries in the world to tax this way. The only other country to tax based on citizenship is Eritrea (a small, war-torn country on the horn of Africa) which implemented citizenship-based taxation as a way to pay back war debt.

Income tax as we know it has been a part of American life since 1913.

In addition to US citizens, Green Card Holders and other individuals who spend substantial time in the United States are also subject to US taxation. (More on that below.)

Filing thresholds determine whether you need to file. The thresholds for taxpayers living in the US are the same as for US taxpayers overseas. This also applies to Digital Nomads.

The filing thresholds for 2021 are:

Filing Status	Gross Income
Single (under age 65)	$12,550
Married Filing Jointly (under age 65)	$25,100
Married Filing Separately (any age)	$5
Head of Household (under age 65)	$18,800

If you are self-employed and earned $400 or more in self-employment income, you also have to file. Furthermore, there are other circumstances where you should file a tax return, even though your income is below the thresholds.

As a US taxpayer living overseas, your worldwide income is subject to taxation. This means that income from a foreign country must be included in your gross income when determining whether you need to file.

Any income earned in a foreign currency must be converted to US dollars. You can use the monthly or yearly average exchange rates or the rate on the specific day of the transaction. Any reputable source, such as the IRS website or Oanda, can be used for the exchange rate. You must use the same exchange rate calculation consistently throughout your tax return, meaning if you use the monthly average for your salary, you must also use the monthly average for calculating your other foreign income and expenses. That being said, you are allowed to choose your exchange rate calculations every year, so it can change from year to year.

Penalties And Fines For Non-Compliance

Penalties for not filing US taxes or filing incorrectly can be steep. Mistakes can happen to anyone, and new expats are especially vulnerable to being unaware of or misunderstanding their obligations.

Generally speaking, the IRS applies three types of penalties:

- Late filing penalties: For tax returns filed after the deadline, the IRS imposes a penalty of 5% of the amount of tax owed per month, for a total of up to 25%. For expats, the penalty starts accumulating on June 16. If the failure to file is deemed fraudulent then the penalty can be increased to up to 75% of the amount of tax owed.
- Late payment penalties: For tax payments made after the original deadline, there is a penalty of 0.5% of the tax owed for each month that the tax is not paid in full, for a total of up to 25%. It starts accumulating on June 16 for Americans abroad.
- Interest accrued on late payments: In addition to paying a penalty for paying late, you have to pay interest on the amount owed starting on April 16, regardless of whether you are an expat or not. The interest rate is the nearest full percentage point of the Federal short-term rate for that calendar quarter, plus 3%. The interest rate is set and applied every quarter.

For example, you owe $20,000 in taxes. You miss the expat tax deadline on June 15 and do not request an extension. If one month later, on July 15, you still have not paid your taxes, you incur $1,000 for late filing and $100 for late payment, and $65.68 in interest on top of the $20,000 you owe. Five months later, you owe $5,000 for failing to file and $600 in late payment penalties, plus $217.56 in interest, for a total of $25,817.56. The exact amount of interest owed depends on the rate set each quarter. You can also be assessed a significant underpayment penalty of 20%. Keep in mind that this is a very simplified example. Other factors could also affect the calculation.

Furthermore, failing to file a tax return is a federal crime that may result in more fines and even jail time. Not even celebrities are safe from jail time or fines. Martha Stewart, Wesley Snipes, and Stephen Baldwin all spent time in jail after being convicted of tax charges.

You can see how quickly this adds up. Fortunately, the IRS offers programs to get back into compliance that can reduce or completely eliminate the penalties. More about that in Chapter 11.

It is also important to note, if you are late on one year of filing, you may qualify for administrative relief from penalties for failing to file a tax return, pay on time, and/or to deposit taxes when due under the IRS First Time Penalty Abatement policy if the following are true:

- You didn't previously have to file a return or you have no penalties for the 3 tax years prior to the tax year in which you received a penalty.
- You filed all currently required returns or filed an extension of time to file.
- You have paid, or arranged to pay, any tax due.

Tax violations can also create other issues. You may be unable to renew your passport, or it may be revoked if your owed taxes exceed $50,000. And if that is not enough, US citizens abroad may lose out on significant exclusions and deductions that could have brought their US tax bill to zero.

Penalties For Business Owners

Business owners abroad also need to be aware of their obligations. C Corporations file their tax return on Form 1120. The late filing penalty for a C Corp may be penalized 5% of the unpaid tax for each month (or part of a month) that the return is overdue, for a total of up to 25% of the unpaid tax. The minimum penalty for a late C Corp return that is more than 60 days late is the amount of tax due or $435, whichever is less. This can be waived if the C Corp can show reasonable cause for failing to file on time. C Corps that pay their taxes late can be penalized ½ of 1% of the unpaid tax for each month or part of a month that the tax is not paid. This penalty has a max of 25% of the unpaid tax amount.

S Corps that fail to file Form 1120S on time but do not owe taxes, can be penalized $210 per shareholder per month or part month that the return is late or that information is missing. If tax is due, then the S Corp can be penalized 5% of the unpaid balance per month or partial month for a total of up to 25%. The penalty for late payment of taxes for an S Corp is the same as for C Corps.

The IRS will also fine foreign corporations that have a presence in the US and fail to file a return. The penalty for failing to file is 5% of the unpaid tax for each month or part of a month that the return is late, with a maximum of 25%. The minimum penalty for a return that is over 60 days late is the amount of tax due or $435. The penalty for late payment is the same as for a C Corp or S Corp. In addition, owners of foreign corporations that are required to file Form 5471 will be automatically fined $10,000 for late submission.

A company that owes taxes and fails to file will be penalized 5% of the unpaid tax amount for every half month or month that the return is late. As with individual returns, the failure to file penalty is limited to 25% of the tax bill.

Again, you may qualify for first time offender relief for your business as detailed above.

Green Card Holders

Even as a Green Card holder, it's not enough to simply leave the country to get out of your US tax obligations. Individuals who have permanent residency that allows them to work and live in the United States, also known as a "Green Card", are subject to US taxation regardless of where they live. The United States taxes Green Card holders the same way as US citizens. Even when they move back to their place of citizenship, Green Card holders remain US taxpayers until they give up their Green Card. Fortunately, specific rules apply to Green Card holders that can help them eliminate or significantly reduce their US tax burden while living abroad, though this can be complicated.

Green Card holders should also take their immigration plans into account when filing US tax returns while living outside the US. If they elect to file as a non-resident and file a 1040NR, this can ultimately disrupt their path to citizenship. Tax treaties may alleviate some or most of this burden, however, utilizing a tax treaty could also affect your immigration status. You should work with a tax attorney or accountant and with your immigration attorney to determine the best approach for your situation.

If you eventually decide to give up your Green Card, you need to formally turn it in at a US embassy. If you simply let it expire, the US government will continue to consider you a US person for tax purposes, even though you are no longer a resident for immigration purposes. This can be a "worst of both worlds" situation as you no longer enjoy the benefits of US residency and are still incurring US taxation. If you are a long-term Green Card holder, you might also have to pay an exit tax before renouncing.

Other People Who Meet The Substantial Presence Test

Spending too much time in the US as a non-citizen or Green Card holder can make you a tax resident. The Substantial Presence Test works like this: You are a tax resident of the United States if you were in the US 31 days or more in the current year and 183 days total in the current year and preceding two years. However, days from the previous two years are calculated in a discounted way.

In the previous year, each day only equals ⅓ of a day. So, three days in the US last year counts as one day for the purposes of the Substantial Presence Test.

In the year before last, each day is only equal to ⅙ of a day. This means that every six days spent in the US during the year before the last count as one day for this test.

In real life, that could look like this: In 2021, an individual, for simplicity let's refer to him as Anthony, spent 160 days in the US. Plus, he was in the US for 70 days in 2020 and 53 days in 2019.

For the purposes of the Substantial Presence Test, Anthony has spent 192 days in the United States [160 + (70/3) + (53/6)] = 192. This puts him significantly over the threshold. He needs to file a US tax return as a resident. If he had left the US just 10 days earlier in the current year, he would've avoided becoming a tax resident in 2021. This is a very simplified and fictional example. Additional factors could also affect the calculation.

For example, Anthony can try to qualify for a closer connection to his home country by filing. By claiming the closer connection test, he will only be taxed on his US-sourced income (not his worldwide income) and avoid other additional lengthy disclosures.

In the case where Anthony is over the 183-day mark in 2021, he can still get out of filing a US resident 1040 tax return, but the process is more complicated and lengthier. If he is a resident of a tax treaty country, he may be able to use the tie breaker rules of the tax treaty to get out of being a US tax resident. It is recommended to work with an advisor on this treaty disclosure.

Tax Benefits For Expats

The idea of citizenship-based taxation can be intimidating, especially for first-time expats. After all, a hefty US tax bill following you around the world is far from ideal. But, with strategy and planning, Americans overseas can reduce or eliminate their US tax burden while staying in compliance. US expats have many tax benefits, such as:

- Excluding income from taxation with the Foreign Earned Income Exclusion (FEIE)
- Claiming the Foreign Housing Exclusion or Deduction for living expenses to help reduce taxes
- Applying the Foreign Tax Credit (FTC) to offset US tax
- Using applicable tax treaty benefits to exclude other income from US taxation
- Structuring your affairs in different ways to achieve tax optimization

With these exclusions, deductions, and credits, many US expats can reduce or even eliminate their US tax burden. And it can all be done completely legally. We explain all of the tax benefits of being an expat in more detail in the coming chapters.

You can only benefit from these tax breaks for expats by filing your US tax return and filing it correctly.

Chapter 3: The Foreign Earned Income Exclusion

The United States taxes based on citizenship. This means that regardless of how long a US taxpayer is abroad or where their income is earned, they need to file a federal tax return if they meet the filing threshold. The threshold can be as low as $5 for married filing separately. For self-employed individuals, net earnings from self-employment of $400 or more meet the filing threshold. For more about being self-employed abroad visit Chapter 13.

Citizenship-based income taxation of overseas Americans dates back to the Civil War and the original goal of the legislation was to make citizens abroad pay extra taxes because they had failed to personally contribute to the efforts of the Union.

Fortunately for expats, the Foreign Earned Income Exclusion (FEIE) was created in its modern form in the 1980s.

What Is The Foreign Earned Income Exclusion And How Does It Work?

The Foreign Earned Income Exclusion (FEIE) is one of the most important strategies for saving on taxes. With the FEIE, Americans abroad can exclude up to just over $100,000 of earned income from federal income tax. (Earned income includes wages, salary, tips, self-employment income. It does not include unearned income such as dividends and interest from investments, pension income, social security, rental income, etc. This type of income is not earned income and cannot be excluded under the FEIE).

This means that an expat who is earning approximately $100,000 and is filing as single could potentially save around $20,000 in income tax (an income in that range would be in the 24% tax bracket. The actual effective tax rate is lower than 24% due to deductions and lower tax rates on the first part of the income).

The exclusion amount increases annually based on inflation. In 2021, eligible expats can earn $108,700 tax-free. Married couples can claim up to $217,400 if both spouses are eligible for the FEIE.

If both spouses qualify independently for the FEIE, they each can claim up to the yearly maximum amount on their separate IRS Form 2555. If only one spouse qualifies, then only that spouse can claim the exclusion and only on their own income. The other spouse cannot claim the FEIE and must include all their income on their US tax return. You can still file jointly even if only one spouse qualifies for FEIE.

The Foreign Earned Income Exclusion is not automatic. Americans who live abroad must claim it by submitting Form 2555. The savings potential of the FEIE and the Foreign Housing Exclusion or Deduction (more on this soon) mean that many expats will benefit from submitting Form 2555 and claiming the FEIE. IRS Form 2555 is optional, not required. In fact, in some cases, US expats choose not to use it because they may be able to save more with other tax provisions, such as the Foreign Tax Credit.

Prorating The FEIE

The FEIE also is prorated for the number of qualifying days. This is usually only important during your first year and during the year you return to the US (if you decide to do so at some point). During your first year abroad when you are presumably a resident of the United States for part of the year and a resident of a foreign country for the other part of the year, you cannot simply claim the full Foreign Earned Income Exclusion of $108,700. Instead, you must calculate the number of days in the tax year that you qualified for the FEIE and then prorate the FEIE amount accordingly (this is actually an area where we see a lot of mistakes when we review expat tax returns prepared either DIY or by tax accountants not familiar with expat taxes).

In simplified terms, to prorate the FEIE, divide the FEIE threshold by 365. This will give you the daily value of the FEIE. Next, multiply the daily value by the number of days you were abroad. This will give you the amount that you can exclude with the FEIE during the year.

For physical presence test, you can add back days of the 35 that were not spent in the US to increase your exclusion. However, any income earned in the US on these days is still taxable. This simply increases the exclusion and benefits you if you earned over the exclusion on the days you were actually abroad.

Let's go over a simplified example to illustrate this concept. The FEIE threshold for 2021 is $108,700, so we will divide this by the number of days in the year ($108,700/365=$297.80). In other words, as long as you are eligible, you could exclude $297.80 per day you are abroad. Next, multiply that by the number of days you were in a foreign country. If you left the US on March 15 to live abroad and for the year, you spent 280 days overseas, then you could exclude about $83,384 from taxes ($297.80 x 280=$83,384). In an actual tax return, this calculation is more complex, as other factors such as the sliding day provision and more also play a role.

How To Qualify For The Foreign Earned Income Exclusion

Not all Americans abroad qualify for the Foreign Earned Income Exclusion. To claim the FEIE, individuals must:

1. Have earned income abroad ("Foreign Earned Income")
2. Have a tax home in a foreign country
3. Pass the physical presence test or the bona fide residence test

A quick note on Green Card holders. They are eligible to claim the FEIE if they meet the above requirements and pass the physical presence test. The situation is slightly more complicated if they want to use the bona fide residence test. Green Card holders can only use the bona fide residence test if they are a citizen or national of a country that has a tax treaty with the US.

Let's look at each of these requirements in more detail:

Foreign Earned Income

Foreign earned income is income earned for performing services outside of the United States. It does not matter whether a US company or a foreign company pays the income, nor if they pay to a US or a foreign bank account. The key for the foreign earned income is that the taxpayer is abroad while earning it, even if they receive a W-2 or Form 1099 for this income. Earned income includes wages, salaries, year-end bonuses, taxable benefits, and self-employment income received while working in a foreign country. The most important factor is that the services are performed abroad.

Some income doesn't qualify though. The following do not qualify as foreign earned income:
- Capital gains
- Dividends
- Interest
- Rental income
- Pension & Social Security
- IRA distributions
- Annuities
- Income earned while working on US soil

Income earned in international waters does not qualify either. This can have a huge impact on the tax return of individuals who work or travel on cruises, join the nomad cruise, or other vessels. In this case, establishing bona fide residency in a foreign country may help claim a portion of the FEIE.

Finally, income earned while working in restricted countries such as Cuba, North Korea, Iran, and others does not qualify for the FEIE.

Tax Home In A Foreign Country

Your tax home is your regular or principal place of business and employment, regardless of where your family residence is. You can have more than one tax home per year. (This is important for digital nomads. More about their specific tax situation in Chapter 14.)

Puerto Rico and other US possessions are not considered foreign countries and cannot be used as a tax home for the purposes of the FEIE. Puerto Rico has other tax incentives instead.

Physical Presence Test Vs. Bona Fide Residence In A Foreign Country

The IRS offers two options to qualify for the Foreign Earned Income Exclusion, the Physical Presence Test and the Bona Fide Residence Test. While they are both good options, Bona Fide Residency is often preferred by those who qualify. However, for first year expats and those who live nomadically, the Physical Presence Test may be their only option.

Physical Presence Test

To pass the physical presence test, an expat needs to be physically present in an eligible foreign country or countries for 330 full days in any 365-day period. It sounds simple but calculating this can be surprisingly complex.

In addition, the IRS is strict about how the physical presence test is calculated. This test offers no leeway. If an individual overstays their presence in the US by one day or even a few hours, they fail the physical presence test and lose the entire FEIE.

When evaluating the physical presence test, the IRS looks at whether you spent 330 full days in eligible foreign countries during a 12-month period, not whether you spent less than 35 days in the United States.

A full day abroad is 24 hours, from midnight to midnight. If you arrive in a foreign country at 2:00 pm local time, your first full day abroad does not start until after midnight. The 10 hours between 2:00 pm and midnight count as part of a day in the US, even though you are in a foreign country.

The requirement to be in an eligible foreign nation also introduces some interesting complications. For the purposes of the physical presence test, certain countries, such as Cuba, North Korea, and Iran, do not qualify.

In addition, international waters and airspace do not constitute a foreign country, so they cannot be counted as a part of a full day abroad. Expats who need to take transatlantic or transpacific flights to reach the United States need to be aware that time spent traveling through international airspace means less time spent in a foreign country, which could reduce the amount of time available to spend in the states.

Connecting travel through the US can also have an impact if the layover is too long. If you are in transit between two points outside of the United States and are physically present in the United States for less than 24 hours, then you are not treated as present in the United States. The IRS treats US airports during international transit as international airspace for the purpose of the FEIE. While transit time of less than 24 hours does not count as a day in the States, it neither counts as a day in a foreign country.

For example, when flying from Tokyo to Mexico City with a six-hour layover in LAX, the time in Los Angeles is not considered time in the US. It is treated as time spent traveling over areas not within any foreign country.

As you can see, tracking physical presence can become complicated quickly.

In certain cases, physical presence may need to be tracked down to the hour. One client, Jane, worked on a cruise ship. During the previous year, Jane had spent the majority of her time on a cruise ship or in Colombia (in fact, due to her ties in Colombia, she qualified to be a bona fide resident there--more on this soon). But she had filed her taxes as if she was still living in the United States. When she realized her mistake, she approached us for assistance.

However, the tax laws for cruise ships are very specific. Depending on whether the ship is in international waters or within the waters of a foreign country, income is taxed differently.

To amend her return, our team tracked the movements of the cruise ship down to the hour so that we could see where Jane had spent each day. With this information, we were able to determine what income was taxable (in US and international waters) and what was not (when she was in a foreign port and traveling in the waters of a foreign country).

Finally, using a little-known ruling called the Roger's Case, we argued to the IRS that they owed her a refund. In the end, Jane received a refund of nearly $10,000.

In short, the physical presence test can be complex. Carefully track physical presence and include a few buffer days in case of travel complications or delays. Overstaying can be a costly mistake.

Another important factor is what constitutes a 12-month period. These 12 months do not have to be a calendar year. It can be any consecutive 12-month period that starts or ends in the tax year. For example, from June 2020 to May 2021. This is especially useful for expats who move abroad mid-year.

In fact, many people use the Physical Presence Test during their first year abroad. Then, once established abroad they may switch to the Bona Fide Residence Test, if they qualify.

However, this isn't an option for everyone. For example, expats on assignment won't qualify for Bona Fide Residence because they have an intention to return to the United States.

Due to the coronavirus pandemic in 2020, the IRS provided a waiver of time requirements for certain US taxpayers. Due to COVID-19, many expats are spending extended time in the US in 2020. Because the world is experiencing these adverse conditions, some US expats can request an adverse conditions waiver as a reason for not passing the Physical Presence Test or Bona Fide Residence Test in 2020.

Bona Fide Residence Test

The Bona Fide Residence Test is for individuals who have established their residence outside of the United States and are intending to stay abroad. It is not automatically granted by living or working outside of the US.

In general, bona residency means that the taxpayer has established a home in a foreign country for an indefinite period. This goes beyond having a foreign address - it means the expat has adopted the foreign country on a social and cultural level. In short, it should be your home overseas. You must have lived there for one entire tax year and have no immediate intentions of returning to live in the US permanently.

First year expats may still be able to claim bona fide residency by filing a special extension delaying their filing until the January after they have completed their first full year abroad, or they can make an amendment to retroactively claim the first partial year abroad after they've completed an entire tax year abroad.

If you go to a country for a temporary period and plan to return to the United States, then you do not qualify for bona fide residency. For example, expats who are on a temporary assignment cannot claim bona fide residency.

A bona fide resident must be able to prove that their center of interests has moved to that country. Those ties can include the following:

- Residency visa or ID (this should be a non-tourist visa)
- Driver's license
- Bank account(s)
- Local employment
- Travel records showing significant time spent in the country
- Rented or purchased home
- Health insurance and potentially other types of insurance (homeowners, renters, life insurance)
- Utility bills
- Local taxes
- Family ties
- Children enrolled in local schools and activities
- Receipts for local expenditures
- Transport, such as a car in the country
- Will registered locally
- Memberships in local clubs, organizations, gyms, libraries, and churches
- Hiring of local professionals and doctors
- Shipping bills and receipts to the foreign country

Not every bona fide resident will fulfill all of the above criteria. This should only serve as a guideline of what may be included. The IRS does not provide any official guidance or "checklist" on what constitutes bona fide residence.

Instead, the Bona Fide Residence Test is subjective and without a fixed definition. In the case of an audit, the IRS evaluates each Bona Fide Residence Test on an individual basis. Both your words and your actions matter, but if the two are in conflict, the IRS will give more weight to your actions.

Because of this, keeping careful records is essential. Keep records of any receipts, bills, or correspondence associated with the above documents.

The Bona Fide Residence Test is a popular option for those who qualify. Expats who are eligible for Bona Fide Residency are not as limited with regards to the number of days they can spend in the US as under the Physical Presence Test. While the number of days spent in the US should be reasonable there is not a specified limit. Of course, with this flexibility also comes responsibility. For instance, the IRS would seriously question your Bona Fide Resident status if you were spending 6 months of the year in the US. We generally recommend spending no more than 3 months of the year in the United States.

Once you qualify you remain a resident of that country for US tax purposes until you give up your residency.

IRS Waiver Of Time Requirement Due To COVID

Due to the coronavirus pandemic in 2020, many expats spent more time in the US in 2020 than they had planned. Under normal circumstances, this would jeopardize their eligibility for the FEIE because they wouldn't be able to meet the time requirements. Fortunately, the IRS provided a waiver of time requirements for certain US taxpayers.

The waiver applies to certain countries and has specific effective dates for those countries. If you left one of the countries on or after the effective date of that country, you can meet the Bona Fide Residence Test or Physical Presence Test for 2020 without meeting the minimum time requirement. While you could still qualify for the FEIE under the waiver, despite spending more time in the States, you must prorate the exclusion based on the actual number of days spent in foreign countries in 2020.

How To Use The Foreign Earned Income Exclusion (With Example)

Let's look at two examples that illustrate the benefits of the Foreign Earned Income Exclusion. Of course, these are simplified examples that focus only on the FEIE.

A US taxpayer, let's call her Jennifer, lives in Mexico City, Mexico. She is employed remotely by a company and earned $75,000 in 2021. The FEIE limit for 2021 is $108,700. Jennifer is using the Bona Fide Residence test and lived abroad during the entire 2021 tax year. Because Jennifer passes the Bona Fide Residence test she is eligible for the full FEIE and can exclude up to $108,700 (2021) from taxes using the FEIE. Jennifer excludes all of her income from US federal income taxes and owes $0. Remember, Jennifer must still file a tax return and claim the FEIE on Form 2555. Now, if Jennifer has other passive income in addition to her salary, she might owe US taxes on that income.

Here's another simplified example. An expat named Matthew works for a tech company in Singapore and earns $150,000. He only went back to the US for a two-week holiday, so he spent 350 days in foreign countries during the 2021 tax year. His wife also works in Singapore, but she goes back to the States more often and does not qualify for the FEIE. Only Matthew can claim the FEIE and only on his income. Because he only went to the US for two weeks, he passed the physical presence test. He didn't work while on holiday in the States, so claims the full FEIE amount of $108,700 (2021). The remaining $41,300 of his salary cannot be excluded. It would be subject to income tax unless he can claim a different credit, exclusion, or deduction, which he likely can. Living in Singapore, Matthew is paying local taxes and also has high rental housing costs that are eligible for the Foreign Housing Exclusion. More on this in Chapter 4 and Chapter 5.

Note that Matthew did not have to prorate his income because he spent more than 330 days abroad and was on vacation during his time in the US, not working. If he had been working and earning income in the US, he would have needed to pro-rate his income.

Common Mistakes When Claiming The FEIE

There are some nuances when it comes to the Foreign Earned Income Exclusion. Below are the most common mistakes.

1. Not Prorating The Exclusion Properly

When using the FEIE, expats need to prorate the exclusion amount if they worked in the United States during the year. Even though the maximum exclusion of the FEIE is $108,700 for 2021, you can only exclude income earned while you were abroad. This means that income earned while you are in the US cannot be included in your FEIE exclusion.

For example, imagine you earned $150,000 in 2021 and did not spend any time working in the US. If you passed the physical presence test, you should be able to exclude the full FEIE amount. So, no pro-rating is necessary. If you were a bona fide resident, you would also get to exclude the FEIE amount, even if you spent 3 months in the US. However, if you worked in the US during those 3 months, that income would be taxable.

This comes up for people who earn significantly more than the FEIE threshold but spend a lot of time in the US. They still get the full exclusion because they're bona fide residents, they just cannot exclude that income earned in the US.

Pro-rating is especially important for first year expats. As most expats move abroad during the year, not on January 1st, their FEIE needs to be prorated based on the amount of time spent abroad.

2. Calculating Taxes On Income That Exceeds The Foreign Earned Income Exclusion

Income that exceeds the FEIE threshold, is taxed at the rate for your total income, as if the FEIE didn't exist. For example, an individual with taxable income of $150,000 would be in the 24% tax bracket. If the taxpayer qualifies for the entire FEIE of $108,700 (2021, single or married filing separately), then the remaining $41,300 are taxed at the 24% tax rate, not at the lower tax rate that would apply to a regular income of $42,000.

Fortunately, you may be able to claim other deductions, exclusions, or credits to further lower your tax liability.

3. Overlooking Related Exclusions And Deductions

Expats who claim the FEIE (and have excess foreign earned income) can often use additional tax benefits, such as the Foreign Housing Exclusion or Deduction and the Foreign Tax Credit, to further reduce their tax burden.

The Foreign Housing Exclusion or Deduction is a way for expats to exclude or deduct certain foreign housing expenses (such as rent and some utilities) from their taxable income. More about the Foreign Housing Exclusion and Deduction in Chapter 4.

The Foreign Tax Credit is a dollar-for-dollar credit for foreign taxes paid. While this can create tax savings for anyone who pays foreign taxes, the benefits are greatest for those who live in high-tax countries. Chapter 5 explains the Foreign Tax Credit in detail.

Expats who have income that exceeds the FEIE and don't claim these exclusions, deductions, and credits may incur significant unnecessary taxes. We have amended hundreds of returns filed by US based accountants to correct extra taxes paid on income that exceeded the FEIE.

4. Taking The Foreign Tax Credit On Income That Was Already Excluded With The Foreign Earned Income Exclusion

If you make $150,000 and exclude $100,000 with the FEIE, you can only use the Foreign Tax Credit for the foreign tax you paid on the non-excluded $50,000. You cannot claim a credit for foreign tax paid on the entire $150,000.

If you claimed the FEIE and the Foreign Tax Credit on the same income, you would be double counting or counting the same income twice.

This also applies when using the FEIE and the Foreign Housing Exclusion or Deduction. The Foreign Housing Exclusion or deduction can only be used on income that exceeds the FEIE.

5. Not Leaving Enough Non-Excluded Income For IRA Contributions

Often, Americans abroad may want to continue contributing to their IRA after moving abroad. This can be difficult because you need non-excluded earned income to make IRA contributions. An expat who excluded all of their income from taxes with the FEIE would be unable to contribute to an IRA because they do not have any non-excluded income.

Individuals in this situation have a few options. If the expat's income exceeds the FEIE threshold, then this income can be used to contribute to an IRA. Even if your income does not exceed the FEIE threshold you might still be able to contribute to an IRA. Income earned during time spent in the USA, maybe during a business trip, is not foreign earned and therefore cannot be excluded under the FEIE. You can use this non-excluded income for IRA contributions. We discuss investment and retirement planning when abroad further in Chapter 10.

6. Reporting Around Owning And Getting Paid From Foreign Corporations

Some people think that because they are being paid by a foreign corporation, they are automatically eligible to exclude their income from US income taxes. Getting paid from a foreign corporation has no impact on Foreign Earned Income Exclusion. It's all about whether the individual passes the tests for the FEIE. Whether the individual is paid by a US or foreign corporation is irrelevant.

Also, remember that while income from a foreign corporation is not subject to FICA or US social security taxes, it could be potentially subject to local taxes.

7. Not Claiming Workdays In The US

As an expat, you need to declare the days that you work in the United States because the income earned during those days is not foreign earned and therefore does not qualify for the FEIE.
This means that you have to pay US income tax on that income. Fortunately, it also means that you have non-excluded income that you can use for IRA contributions. If you are in the US but not working (on vacation), this income is not US taxable income.

8. Claiming The Foreign Earned Income Exclusion When The Foreign Tax Credit Would Be More Beneficial

This mistake is particularly common. Because the Foreign Earned Income can seem simpler, some taxpayers mistakenly choose the FEIE when the Foreign Tax Credit would have been the better choice.

This is especially true for expats who live in high-tax jurisdictions, such as Canada, the United Kingdom, and many Western European countries. Americans abroad who live in high-tax jurisdictions can get a dollar-for-dollar credit for paid foreign taxes. Unlike the FEIE, using the Foreign Tax Credit allows them to contribute to IRAs and to claim the Child Tax Credit. In some cases, they could even receive a refund from the Child Tax Credit.

Another crucial benefit of the Foreign Tax Credit is that unused credits can be saved for use in future years. This represents a significant tax planning opportunity for many expats.

9. Forgetting Self-Employment Taxes

The Foreign Earned Income Exclusion does not reduce self-employment taxes. This means that even though self-employed expats can exclude over $100,000 from income taxes, they still need to pay self-employment taxes including social security and Medicare taxes. More on self-employment taxes in Chapter 12 and Chapter 13.

Chapter 4: The Foreign Housing Exclusion Or Deduction

Foreign housing can be expensive, especially, if you are based in a large city. Cities in Switzerland, Japan, Norway, Denmark, Singapore, and more regularly rank among the most expensive in the world.

Fortunately, expats can offset some of these expenses with the Foreign Housing Exclusion or Deduction.

What Is The Foreign Housing Exclusion Or Deduction And How Does It Work?

The Foreign Housing Exclusion or Deduction allows expats to exclude or deduct from their taxes certain housing expenses, that exceed a set threshold.

This exclusion or deduction offsets some of the cost of living and working abroad. The Foreign Housing Exclusion or Deduction is requested on IRS Form 2555. This is the same form that is used for the Foreign Earned Income Exclusion (FEIE).

The requirements to claim the Foreign Housing Exclusion or Deduction are relatively similar to those for the FEIE. Here they are:

- Claim the Foreign Earned Income Exclusion (FEIE)
- Establish your tax home in a foreign country
- Pass the physical presence or bona fide residence test

- Have eligible foreign housing expenses that exceed the minimum threshold

We explained the first three requirements in Chapter 3: The Foreign Earned Income Exclusion. However, we still need to explain the last requirement.

Exclusion Or Deduction?

US taxpayers abroad who are employed can claim an exclusion for eligible housing costs. They can also claim the exclusion for expenses paid for with employer-provided funds. A common misperception is that "employer-provided amounts" means only employer-paid housing. Instead, it actually includes anything paid to you or paid by your employer for you. For example, if your employer pays for your housing expenses directly, and you never directly handle the funds, that is considered a qualified housing expense. Otherwise, if you are paying the housing expenses directly, then the full amount is considered a qualified housing expense.

Self-employed expats can claim a deduction. The deduction only applies to the amount of housing expenses paid for with self-employment earnings.

To clarify, an exclusion is an amount that does not have to be included in gross income for tax purposes. A deduction lowers your taxable income which means that you will owe less taxes. In some instances, you can receive both the exclusion and deduction.

Foreign Housing Exclusion Limits

The threshold for the Foreign Housing Exclusion or Deduction changes each year based on the limit for the Foreign Earned Income Exclusion. The minimum for the Foreign Housing Exclusion or Deduction is set at 16% of the FEIE limit.

For 2021, the FEIE limit is $108,700. This means that the Foreign Housing minimum threshold is $17,392 in ($108,700 x 16%). In other words, you can only exclude expenses for 2021 that exceeded $17,392.

If you only qualify for the FEIE for part of the year, the threshold will be prorated.

In addition to the threshold, the IRS also limits the maximum amount you can exclude or deduct. The standard maximum is 30% of the Foreign Earned Income Exclusion (FEIE). Therefore, in 2021, the standard maximum is $32,610 ($108,700 x 30%).

If spouses shared the same home but are filing separately then only one can claim the Foreign Housing Exclusion or Deduction.

If you and your spouse live in the same home outside of the US and are filing your taxes jointly, then you calculate your housing expenses together. For more on which filing status might be most beneficial, visit Chapter 9.

As with the minimum, the maximum is prorated based on the number of days during the year that you qualified for the FEIE.

High-Cost Locations

However, housing limits vary. In some cities, the limit is higher depending on differences in foreign housing costs relative to housing costs in the United States. Each year the IRS publishes a list of cities with limits that exceed the standard maximum. As an example, expats in Hong Kong have an exclusion or deduction limit of $114,300 (2021) per year. Expats in Denmark can exclude or deduct up to $43,704 (2021) in housing expenses each year. In Spain, US taxpayers can exclude up to $40,600 (2021) in Barcelona or up to $62,000 (2021) in Madrid. Americans living in Singapore can exclude or deduct up to $84,100 (2021).

Make sure to speak with your accountant or check the IRS list of cities with higher limits each year. If your city does not have an extended limit you must use the general maximum of 30% of the FEIE.

Eligible Housing Expenses

Next, you need to verify that you have qualifying expenses. According to the IRS, only reasonable expenses that you actually paid or incurred qualify for the Foreign Housing Exclusion or Deduction. Reasonable expenses include:

- Rent
- Utilities
- Real and personal property insurance
- Rental of furniture and accessories
- Repairs
- Residential parking
- Non-refundable deposits to secure a lease
- Fair market value of employer-owned housing provided to you

Other expenses may also qualify. However, not all foreign housing costs can be claimed for the Foreign Housing Exclusion or Deduction. According to the IRS, any expenses that are deemed lavish or extravagant are ineligible. Future or expected costs do not qualify. Likewise, if you have employer-provided housing, the value of the property does not qualify for the Foreign Housing Exclusion or Deduction. These costs do not qualify for the Foreign Housing Exclusion or Deduction:

- The cost of a property you purchased and any associated transaction fees
- Domestic labor (cleaning, cooking)
- Television
- Phone bills
- Purchased furniture
- Improvements to a property
- Mortgage payments

If you are unsure of whether an expense qualifies, contact a tax professional to verify.

How To Use The Foreign Housing Exclusion Or Deduction (With Example)

The Foreign Housing Exclusion or Deduction is an excellent savings opportunity for US taxpayers living overseas. In most cases, eligible US taxpayers who have income that exceeds the FEIE threshold will claim the Foreign Housing Exclusion or Deduction next. If they have a remaining US liability, then the Foreign Tax Credit may also be used. (In some cases, it makes more sense to use the Foreign Tax Credit entirely, instead of the FEIE. More about this in the next chapter.)

Typically, expats use this exclusion or deduction to offset their personal housing expenses. For example, a US citizen, let's call him Alex, lives in Mexico City and paid $50,000 in eligible housing expenses during 2021. Mexico City has a foreign housing exclusion or deduction limit of $47,900. Alex can exclude housing expenses that exceed the 2021 threshold of $17,392 up to Mexico City's limit of $47,900 (2021). In Alex's case, he is spending over the location's limit, so he will subtract the threshold from the limit to see how much he can exclude for the year ($47,900 - $17,392 = $30,508). This means that Alex can exclude $30,508 of his foreign housing expenses. Alex is employed so he will take the exclusion, not a deduction. Because Alex is also claiming the Foreign Earned Income Exclusion, he can exclude a total of $139,208 $30,508 + 108,700 = $139,208). (This is a very simplified, fictional example. Additional factors could also affect the calculation).

Some expats even go a step further. If you own a home in a foreign country, you could rent it out (paying tax on the rental income) and live in a rented home. Those rental expenses would qualify for the exclusion or deduction. It could work like this: you live in Hong Kong in an apartment that you own with your family. You decide to move out of the apartment and rent it out. You and your family rent a different apartment to live in. The rent you are receiving from the property you own essentially offsets the rent you're paying in the new place. However, you are able to include the rent you paid in the Foreign Housing Exclusion which, depending on the cost of the apartment and eligible expenses, could result in about $80,000 of tax-free income due to the high housing exclusion in Hong Kong. Of course, you should take into consideration any additional tax that you might pay either locally or to the US on the rental income. This strategy only works if you have sufficient expenses, such as depreciation, associated with the rental property to lower your taxable income from the rental property. If you don't have sufficient expenses, this strategy doesn't offer any benefits. Most of the time, there is not additional tax on rental income in the US due to expenses including depreciation, however there may be tax on that income when the property is sold due to depreciation addback rules.

If you own real estate in the US or abroad, we discuss further savings strategies and reporting requirements in Chapter 10.

Chapter 5: The Foreign Tax Credit

The Foreign Tax Credit is a dollar-for-dollar credit for taxes paid to a foreign government on foreign-sourced income. While the Foreign Earned Income Exclusion (FEIE) excludes foreign earned income from US taxation, the Foreign Tax Credit does not exclude the income. Instead, it reduces the US taxes by applying credit for the taxes already paid abroad. This is especially helpful when living in countries with high tax rates.

Expats who pay eligible foreign taxes can use this credit regardless of whether there is a tax treaty or not (Chapter 6 has further details on tax treaty benefits). Unlike the Foreign Earned Income Exclusion in which one's entire income is excluded, potentially bringing the adjusted gross income to zero, the Foreign Tax Credit makes it easy for expats to contribute to IRAs and claim additional credits such as Child Tax Credit. The Foreign Tax Credit can also create a significant tax planning opportunity through the usage of carryover credits. From a tax strategy perspective, this is one of its largest advantages.

Taxpayers claim the credit on IRS Form 1116, which they file with their tax return.

Can I Claim The Foreign Tax Credit?

The IRS gives tax credits to US taxpayers who have already paid a tax on the income to another country. By claiming these dollar-for-dollar credits, taxpayers can offset taxes paid to a foreign country and limit or avoid double taxation.

However, before you can claim the Foreign Tax Credit, make sure that you have income that was not already excluded from US taxation under the FEIE. You can only claim a Foreign Tax Credit for taxes you paid on non-excluded income. Non-excluded income could be income that exceeds the Foreign Earned Income Exclusion, income that was re-sourced by a treaty, or income that was earned while in the US and therefore did not fall under the FEIE. If you excluded all of your income using the

Foreign Earned Income Exclusion and the Foreign Housing Exclusion or Deduction, then you cannot use the Foreign Tax Credit for tax paid on that income.

To claim a credit for a foreign tax, the tax must meet these requirements:

1. The tax is an income tax, or a tax implemented in place of an income tax
2. The tax must have been "imposed" and was not optional
3. The tax has been paid or accrued
4. Only the amount of foreign tax that you actually owed or accrued qualifies (which could be less than the foreign tax withholding)

The Tax Is An Income Tax Or A Tax Implemented In Place Of An Income Tax

Only some types of foreign taxes qualify for the Foreign Tax Credit. Americans can receive the Foreign Tax Credit for foreign taxes on the following:

- Income
- Wages
- Dividends
- Interest
- Royalties
- War profits
- Excess profits

Income from self-employment and employment both qualify. However, keep in mind when claiming the Foreign Tax Credit that tax credits for general income and passive income are separate. You can only credit one type of income tax to a tax for the same type of income. In other words, only foreign credits for general income can be applied to your US tax liability for general income. Likewise, foreign credits for passive income can only be applied to US taxes for passive income. This means you cannot use a foreign tax credit for the tax you paid on salary to offset US tax due on capital gains. General income most commonly includes income from your salary if you work for an employer or are self-employed. It can also include many other types of income such as pension contributions. Passive income includes income from capital gains, dividends, interest, and rental income.

Some taxes do not qualify. For example, you cannot receive a Foreign Tax Credit for wealth taxes based on net worth. Other types of foreign taxes that cannot be used for the Foreign Tax Credit, include:

- Taxes for which you can only take an itemized deduction
- Taxes on foreign mineral income

- Taxes from international boycott operations
- A portion of taxes on combined foreign oil and gas income
- Taxes of US persons controlling foreign corporations and partnerships who fail to file required information returns
- Taxes related to a foreign tax splitting event
- Social security taxes paid or accrued to a foreign country with which the United States has a social security agreement. For more information about these agreements, visit Chapter 6.

The Tax Must Have Been "Imposed" And Was Not Optional

Simply, if a tax is optional then you cannot claim a credit for it. The tax must be imposed on you by a foreign country, city, region, or province. For example, because the church tax in Germany is optional, it does not qualify for a foreign tax credit. The German solidarity surcharge ("Soli") however does qualify because it is mandatory.

Taxes imposed by the US territories of Puerto Rico or American Samoa also qualify for the Foreign Tax Credit.

The Tax Has Been Paid Or Accrued

The tax has been paid, or it has not yet been paid but it has been accumulating and you are obligated to pay it. As an example, most workers in Singapore pay the majority of their tax bill in the following year. In other words, they will pay most of their 2021 tax bill in 2022. If they claim foreign taxes accrued, it would be the amount based on their 2021 earnings even though they actually pay it next year.

Only The Amount Of Foreign Tax That You Actually Owed Or Accrued Qualifies (Which Could Be Less Than The Foreign Tax Withholding)

You can only claim a credit for the portion of the tax that you were actually required to pay, after taking tax treaties and other remedies into account, even if the foreign tax withholding was higher. Basically, if you paid more than you were legally required to in a foreign country, you have to get it back from the foreign country. You cannot just claim it as a tax credit for the US return .

As an example, if you paid taxes and received or will receive a refund in the foreign country, then this will affect the amount of tax credit you can claim. If $3,000 in taxes were withheld, but you expect to receive a full refund of $3,000 from the foreign government, then the tax is not eligible for the Foreign Tax Credit.

Changes For US Taxpayers In France

Up until 2019, US taxpayers in France faced an issue. The IRS considered taxes paid into the French Contribution Sociale Generalisee (CSG) and Contribution au Remboursement de la Dette Sociate (CRDS) as social taxes that were covered by a totalization agreement between the US and France. Because of this position, expats in France could not claim foreign tax credits on these taxes. Fortunately, in 2019 the two governments agreed that the IRS would accept foreign tax credits for these taxes.

Americans who have paid the CSG and CRDS taxes previously can claim a refund with the IRS. The 10-year period to claim starts the day after the regular due date of the return.

Foreign Tax Credit Carryovers And Carrybacks

The Foreign Tax Credit not only reduces current year income tax. It can also reduce a future tax burden. When you pay higher taxes abroad than you would have in the United States, the Foreign Tax Credit can bring your current year US tax liability down to zero. And you can claim any unused tax credit in future years.

These are called carryovers. Similarly, credits can also be applied to previous tax years. This is called a carryback. Carryovers and carrybacks are used because tax credits can only bring your US tax liability to zero. You cannot get a refund if you paid more foreign tax than you would have paid in the US. You can only save unused Foreign Tax Credit for later. Credits can be carried back to the previous tax year or carried forward up to 10 years into the future. But they can only be used if you have foreign sourced income. You cannot use them against your US sourced income, such as US employment or investment income, if you move back to the US.

Expats can apply these carryover credits later if they move to a low tax jurisdiction (such as Hong Kong or the UAE). Thereby, they reduce their long-term tax obligations.

How To Use The Foreign Tax Credit (With Example)

The Foreign Tax Credit can represent massive savings for US taxpayers who meet the above requirements. It also can create an opportunity to reduce the amount of taxes owed in the future by using carryovers and carrybacks.

Michael is an American citizen who lives and works in Japan. During his time there, his Japanese tax liability has always exceeded his US tax liability. Each year he claims the maximum amount of tax credit, effectively eliminating his US tax burden. Because his Japanese tax bill is significantly higher than his US tax bill, he can carry over his excess foreign tax credit to be used in the future.

After living in Japan for 4 years, he moves to Singapore, a territorial tax jurisdiction. As Michael is earning his income from outside of Singapore, he incurs no Singaporean taxes. However, Michael still needs to consider his US tax burden. First, he claims the Foreign Earned Income Exclusion. This allows him to exclude just over $100,000 of his income from US income taxes. Next, he can exclude about $60,000 in housing expenses in Singapore using the Foreign Housing Exclusion or Deduction (visit Chapter 4 for more on this). However, Michael's income exceeds $160,000 which means he could end up owing US taxes if he doesn't implement other strategies. Fortunately, he can apply his unused foreign tax credit from his time in Japan to eliminate some or all of the remaining tax burden. We'll explain this more soon. For now, just keep in mind that the Foreign Tax Credit not only helps to avoid double taxation, it also can play an important role in your long-term tax strategy.

Should Expats Use The Foreign Tax Credit Or The Foreign Earned Income Exclusion?

Often, US taxpayers living abroad are not sure if the Foreign Earned Income Exclusion (FEIE) or the Foreign Tax Credit (FTC) is better for them. They both have advantages but choosing the wrong one can be costly.

There are many factors to consider before choosing the FTC over the FEIE. Key considerations include:

- Tax rate in the country of residence
- Ability to contribute to retirement plans
- Claiming the child tax credit
- Future plans

Let's look at each of those.

Living In A High Tax Jurisdiction

Often, US Americans living in a high tax country pay higher taxes there than they would have paid in the US. Those expats typically benefit from using the Foreign Tax Credit instead of the FEIE.

However, if an expat has a foreign tax rate that is lower than their US tax rate, they should consider the Foreign Earned Income Exclusion.

The tax rate of your residence country however is not the only factor to consider.

Ability To Contribute To Retirement Plans

To be able to contribute to an IRA, the taxpayer must have non-excluded income. If expats use the FEIE to exclude all their income from income tax, they do not have any non-excluded income left for IRA contributions. So, you might think that you should use the Foreign Tax Credit instead. However, you might still be able to contribute to an IRA when using the Foreign Earned Income Exclusion.

Claiming the FEIE does not preclude expats from making an IRA contribution as long as they have non-excluded income that they can use for the contribution.

For example, if an expat has foreign income that exceeds the FEIE limit, then he has non-excluded income and can contribute. Similarly, income that is not foreign-sourced, for example from working during a business trip in the US, cannot be excluded and therefore can be used for IRA contributions (for more on this visit Chapter 10).

Expats that want to make retirement contributions should discuss their options with an experienced expat tax accountant.

Claiming The Child Tax Credit

Eligible expats can use the Child Tax Credit and the Foreign Tax Credit together. This allows them to reduce their US tax burden even further. In some cases, the Child Tax Credit can bring the tax bill to zero or even result in a refund from the IRS. In 2021, up to $1,400 of the Child Tax Credit is refundable. In order to qualify for the Child Tax Credit, one must have eligible US children (with a social security number) and income under the limit. More on this in Chapter 9.

Future Plans

Your future plans are crucial for deciding between the FEIE or the FTC. If you use the FEIE, and then the next year you decide not to, you revoke the FEIE and cannot take it until the sixth year after the revocation year. This means going five full tax years without taking the FEIE.

Sometimes people default to taking the FEIE and then realize later that the FTC is more optimal in their situation. They then have to consider if they will move to a lower tax burden area in the future or not.

The exclusion can only be revoked through written permission from the IRS. We have revoked the exclusion in certain cases, as well as the opposite by invoking the exclusion through a special appeal process with the IRS.

Expats should be careful when choosing whether to use the FEIE, the Foreign Tax Credit, or both. While the Foreign Tax Credit has many advantages, it is not the right choice for everybody. In fact, in some cases, expats could lose money with the Foreign Tax Credit. Sometimes, the Foreign Earned Income Exclusion is a better choice.

Expats that use the FEIE and the Foreign Housing Exclusion or Deduction to exclude their foreign income from US income tax might still be able to use the Foreign Tax Credit for any income that exceeds the FEIE limits or other non-excluded income.

A careful analysis of each expat's unique tax situation and long-term plan is crucial.

Chapter 6: Tax Treaty Benefits

Tax treaties are an often-overlooked part of tax planning. In fact, forgetting to check for a tax treaty can result in you being taxed twice on the same income. Furthermore, they are complex documents. Misunderstanding or missing a clause can lead to an incorrectly filed tax return and potential penalties (More on penalties in Chapter 1).

Still, when correctly understood, tax treaties are an important part of tax optimization for many US taxpayers abroad. In one case, our team was able to save a client millions of dollars by applying the tax treaty. A few years ago, an Argentine family approached us for tax assistance after their father passed away. During his lifetime, the father had built a multi-million-dollar stock portfolio at a US brokerage firm. When he passed away, the brokerage firm froze his account and argued that as a non-US person who owned stock, the man's family owed the IRS a 40% estate tax. As an FYI, as a non-US citizen or resident, the US can lay claim to inheritance tax on your US "situs" assets (such as US stocks, real estate, partnerships) if the value of these assets is over $60,000 upon your death. During our consultation with the family, we discovered that the father had immigrated from Italy to Argentina as a young man and that he was still an Italian citizen at the time of his passing.

Working directly with the IRS, we were able to establish that the family patriarch was still an Italian citizen and was eligible for an exception under the US-Italy Estate Tax Treaty from the 1940s. By applying for this exemption, the Argentine family protected millions of dollars from estate taxes and preserved their father's assets. (For other non-US persons who have US situs assets, estate taxes can be prevented by owning the assets in a foreign company or a foreign trust).

As you can see, tax treaties can have a significant impact on your tax liability.

Income Tax Treaties

An income tax treaty is an agreement between two countries that outlines different types of income and where they will be taxed. Tax treaties can protect against double taxation in situations where a foreign tax credit would not apply. Each treaty is different, though they may provide exemptions or reduced tax rates for certain types of income, including retirement or pension plans, business income, or reduced withholding rates on passive income such as dividends and interest, and more.

Tax treaties are not only for US expats. They may also cover taxation in a variety of circumstances such as non-resident alien investors in the US, green card holders, and any other situations in which two jurisdictions may claim the right to tax the same income.

The United States has tax treaties with over 60 countries, including most (but not all) popular expat destinations. The list of countries with income tax treaties includes

Australia, Canada, most of Europe, Mexico, China, Japan, and even far-flung places like Kyrgyzstan. However, other popular destinations such as Singapore, Hong Kong, Panama, UAE, Brazil, and Colombia, do not have a tax treaty with the US at this time.

As beneficial as tax treaties can be, they are not always needed to save taxes. For example, if you work and live in Germany, then the tax treaty between the United States and Germany might not be important for you. If all of your income is sourced in Germany and taxed there, then you should be able to eliminate your tax burden with the Foreign Tax Credit, without a need for the tax treaty.

Instead, tax treaties are most crucial in situations where there isn't already prevention against double taxation (such as the Foreign Earned Income Exclusion or Foreign Tax Credit, both explained in earlier chapters).

Taxation Of Social Security And Pensions

Tax treaties can determine which country can tax your social security income or distributions. In which country you have to pay into the social security system is determined by Totalization Agreements (more on this below). American taxpayers who live in countries without tax treaties may need to work with their accountant abroad for tax relief.

For example, a US citizen and retiree who lives in Brazil, let's call her Anne, receives a pension from the US and pays US taxes on her pension income. She also has to pay taxes in Brazil on her income. Between the two countries, Anne is paying almost 50% of her income in taxes. The US does not have a treaty with Brazil and because her pension is US-sourced income, she isn't eligible for the FEIE or the Foreign Tax Credit. To reduce her tax burden, she will need to work with her Brazilian accountant and see if she can get a tax credit in Brazil. Unfortunately, pension income is not eligible for FEIE and, some countries do not give a foreign tax credit but rather view taxes paid to other countries as a deduction against income, which is not as favorable.

Saving Clause

Most US tax treaties are relatively similar. Still, they have differences. Generally, an income tax treaty will cover multiple types of income and confirm where it should be taxed. In addition, the US government includes a saving clause in some treaties.

The saving clause essentially says that the US government retains the right to tax US citizens as if the treaty doesn't exist. This means that, in the eyes of the US government, nothing in the treaty matters for US citizens unless an exception is mentioned in the text.

Generally, there are a handful of exceptions to the saving clause specifically outlined in the treaty. These exceptions allow the treaty to be read as is for both countries, rather than the one-sided reading that the saving clause creates.

Income Re-Sourcing

The re-sourcing clause found in some treaties allows certain types of income that are sourced in one country to be taxed as if it was sourced in another country.

The most common example of this is when someone is working abroad for a foreign company and is sent on a work trip to the US. For example, Jennifer is a US citizen and a resident of Australia for all of 2021. She pays Australian income taxes on her employment income and spends 10 days in the US for a business trip in February. The income earned while in the United States is considered US-sourced and taxed by the IRS. This income is not eligible for the Foreign Earned Income Exclusion or the general Foreign Tax Credit because it was earned in the United States. Because the employer is Australian, the Australian government will also tax it as Australian earned income. Moreover, the Australian government does not provide any relief for the income earned abroad. In short, Jennifer could potentially be taxed twice on this income.

Fortunately, by claiming Article 22 of the US-Australia Treaty, US-sourced income can be re-sourced as foreign-earned and qualify for the Foreign Tax Credit. With this treaty, Jennifer avoided double taxation on the income earned during her US travel.

As an example, US social security benefits paid to a US person living in Canada are re-sourced as Canadian and taxed in Canada as if they were benefits under the Canada Pension Plan. However, under the US-Canada tax treaty, 15% of the social security amount is exempt from Canadian tax. This means that if you receive US Social Security benefits and are a resident of Canada, then Canada will only tax 85% of the benefits you receive. Fortunately, US persons in Canada can also claim a Foreign Tax Credit on their US tax return because the income has been re-sourced as Canadian.

Social Security Totalization Agreements

A totalization agreement is a type of tax treaty that addresses US taxation of Social Security and Medicare taxes. This may seem similar to the income tax treaties discussed above. However, these two types of treaties are different.

Income tax treaties can determine which country can tax your social security income or distributions. On the other hand, totalization agreements determine where you should make social security contributions and where you will pay social security taxes to.

Often, if your country of residence has a totalization agreement with the United States and you are only in the country temporarily, then you can continue contributing to US Social Security. However, there are exceptions. Usually, you will not have a choice about where you will contribute. Rather, it is generally dictated by an agreement between the US and that country. And often, if you are going to spend a couple of years working in a foreign country, you will be required to pay into their social security system. Though, exceptions do, exist. For example, we have seen US citizens who are long-term residents in Italy that only pay into the US system and not the Italian one.

If you can choose where you contribute, check how long you have been contributing to the US social security system. To receive US social security distributions, US taxpayers need to pay into the system for at least 40 quarters (this is equivalent to ten years of contributions). If you are close to this 40-quarter mark, it may be worth continuing your contributions until then so that you can receive US social security distributions upon retirement. Furthermore, if you want to qualify for social security disability, 20 credits need to be earned within the last 10 years (exceptions apply for younger taxpayers). There are ways for expats to still contribute and apply for social security, even with no US income, by showing income on schedule C and paying self-employment tax on this income. In 2022, for example, you earn one credit for each $1,510 in wages or self-employment income. When you've earned $6,040, you've earned your maximum four credits for the year.

Totalization agreements can also apply to self-employed expats. Self-employed US taxpayers need to pay social security even when living abroad. (Though they can reduce it if they form an LLC and elect S Corp status. More on this in Chapter 13). However, in some situations, totalization agreements may exempt self-employed US persons from paying into the US system. The US-Spain totalization agreement is one example of this. The agreement says that if you are self-employed in Spain, you do not need to pay self-employment tax in the United States if you are paying into the Spanish system. Nevertheless, self-employed US expats in Spain still need to notify the IRS that they are paying social security in Spain by obtaining a certificate of coverage from the Spanish authorities.

The situation is similar in Canada. With this agreement, you generally will only pay self-employment tax to the country you are residing in while self-employed, though you will need to obtain a certificate of coverage from the local Canadian office to show the IRS, if requested.

Americans who live in countries that do not have a totalization agreement with the US may end up having to pay into both countries' systems. As an expat hub, this is a common issue for US taxpayers in Costa Rica. Without a totalization agreement between the two countries, in other cases, expats are subject to both US Social Security and Costa Rican Caja on the same income. Similar situations can occur in other popular destinations for Americans abroad such as Singapore, Hong Kong, Panama, and many countries in Western Europe.

Some countries without a totalization agreement with the US may let you opt-out of their social security plan if you demonstrate that you are paying into a foreign plan. Hong Kong, among others, offers this option to individuals who meet certain requirements. Still, be sure to consult with an accountant or tax attorney in that country before making a decision.

Fortunately, there is a silver lining. When a country does not have a Social Security Totalization Agreement with the United States, the social security tax of that country is considered an income tax for Foreign Tax Credit purposes.

As a reminder, the US has Totalization Agreements with some countries that it has no tax treaty with.

Many American taxpayers are unaware that they could potentially save money with a tax treaty. While income tax treaties and totalization agreements are the two types of tax treaties that are most useful for expats, other types of treaties, such as the Germany-US Estate and Gift Tax Treaty, do exist and can help alleviate double taxation.

Finally, as a reminder, keep in mind that these treaties are highly complex and technical. You should not take any single paragraph of a treaty by itself. It's important to review the entire treaty (including the savings clause), as well as the protocol and technical explanations.

Chapter 7: Reporting Foreign Assets And Bank Accounts

While living abroad you will likely open a foreign bank account and accumulate some foreign assets or investments. A foreign bank account may be needed for local transactions or you may live in a country that requires you to set up a foreign pension. Or even when living in the US, you may have a foreign bank account or ownership of a foreign corporation. Having a foreign bank account also establishes that you are a bona fide resident of a country, which will further your case in the event of an audit.

Different types of foreign accounts and assets may trigger filing requirements with the United States Department of Treasury or the IRS. Depending on the type of asset, you may need to file different forms.

Moreover, this is an area where US persons need to be especially careful. In the last 10 years, there has been a push around the world for countries to share more information. The implementation of FATCA and the Common Reporting Standard (CRS) show that the US government takes foreign financial account reporting seriously.

FBAR For Foreign Financial Accounts

The FBAR, or Foreign Bank Account Report, is one of the most important reporting forms for individuals with foreign accounts. Whether you live abroad or in the US, having a foreign bank account can be useful. But a foreign bank account can also come with unexpected reporting obligations.

Whether your account is for making and receiving payments locally, for a pension, business, or another reason, it could trigger a filing requirement in the US with the Department of the Treasury. Failure to come forward and report voluntarily can result in severe penalties if the accounts are discovered by the Treasury or the IRS.

Who Needs To File An FBAR?

If you have any accounts at financial institutions outside of the United States, you are considered a foreign financial account holder. Many Americans mistakenly believe that the FBAR only applies to foreign bank accounts. However, other types of foreign financial accounts like pension accounts, are also a part of FBAR and could put you over the threshold. Any financial (deposit or custodial) accounts held at foreign financial institutions or any financial accounts held at a foreign branch of a US financial institution are reportable on the FBAR. In several instances, we have seen people whose foreign bank accounts are below the FBAR's $10,000 threshold so they haven't filed. Then when we ask about their foreign investment and pension accounts that put them way beyond the threshold. If not corrected this type of error can result in stiff penalties.

Keep in mind that FBAR filing requirements cover all "US Persons." This includes US citizens and US residents, as well as US entities. US entities include corporations, partnerships, LLCs, or trusts created under the laws of the United States. Your relationship to and the funds held in the foreign financial account will determine whether you need to file the FBAR.

Simply, you need to submit the FBAR before the due date if:

- You have signature authority over or financial interest in a foreign financial account, and
- The total value of those accounts is over $10,000 at any one time during the year

So, what do these terms mean?

Signature Authority:

If you provide instructions to the financial institution in written or other forms, you have signature authority. Signature authority is not limited to written communications according to the IRS. Furthermore, whether you have ever exercised your ability to control the account is irrelevant.

With signature authority, the assets in the account may not even be yours and your name may not even be on the account. Still, if you are authorized to access the account and make transactions i.e., check-signing authority, you have "signature authority with no financial interest". This could be a corporate account at your place of employment or an account that belongs to a family member. For example, your elderly parents have given you power of attorney over their bank account in Canada, but you have never exercised your power of attorney on the account. You must file the FBAR since you have signature authority over the account.

Financial Interest:

You have a financial interest in an account and might need to file the FBAR if:

- You are the owner or holder of the account
- Another person is the owner or holder of the account, but they act and manage the account on your behalf

It is important to keep in mind that you can have financial interest even if the account is not in your name. For example, you are a US citizen. Your brother Michael maintains accounts in Mexico on your behalf. The accounts are in Michael's name, but he only accesses the accounts as instructed by you. In this situation, you have a financial interest in the account, and you have to report this account if you meet the FBAR reporting thresholds. If Michael is also a US citizen or resident, he must also file an FBAR.

Total Value Of Your Accounts Is Over $10,000 At Any Time During The Year

Finally, if the combined value of your foreign financial accounts exceeds $10,000 US Dollars at any one time during the year, then you need to file an FBAR.

For example, imagine that on August 15, you have one foreign account with $5,000 and another foreign account with $6,000. The total during that day surpasses the $10,000 threshold and you need to file the FBAR. You need to include any foreign financial accounts that you have a financial interest in or a signature authority over in this calculation. We explain more about financial interest and signature authority in Chapter 7.

In addition, when making this calculation, you need to convert any foreign currency to USD (US Dollars) using the Bureau of the Fiscal Service's end of year exchange rates (not the average exchange rate). The Bureau of the Fiscal Service is a part of the Treasury department.

Accounts With A Foreign Spouse

One common area of confusion is how Americans should report their non-resident alien (NRA) spouse's foreign bank accounts. Your spouse is a non-resident alien if they do not have US citizenship nor US residency and they hold citizenship in another country (and you do not elect to file jointly with them on your US tax return). You do not need to report your NRA spouse's foreign accounts on the FBAR if both of the following are true:

1. You do not have signing authority, and
2. Your name is not associated with the accounts.

If you have signing authority or if your name is associated with the account, you must include the accounts in your FBAR report. This includes reporting joint accounts with your NRA spouse.

FBAR For Business Owners

Though many people think the FBAR is only applicable to individuals, it also applies to US entities. A US entity is any corporation, partnership, LLC, trust, or estate formed under US law.

The requirements for filing are the same for individuals and entities. Your US entity must submit the FBAR if it has a financial interest or signature authority on foreign financial accounts with an aggregate value greater than $10,000 during the year.

Whether you will need to submit an FBAR for your US entity depends on the amount of voting power you have, the number of shares, and several other factors. How your ownership is measured depends on the type of entity.

Subsequent entities may also trigger FBAR requirements. If your US parent entity has more than 50% ownership of a subsequent foreign entity which has a foreign financial account, then the US parent entity needs to file an FBAR reporting that account. Whether your entity has more than 50% ownership can depend on a variety of factors. These factors include the number of voting shares, percentage of profits or capital, and more.

It is key that you are aware of other entities owned by your US entity. These subsequent entities may make your business liable to file the FBAR. Depending on the situation, the parent entity and the subsequent entity may be able to file a consolidated FBAR.

How To File An FBAR (Foreign Bank Account Report)

Many people mistakenly assume that the FBAR is filed with the IRS. The Foreign Bank Account Report (FBAR) is actually submitted to the Financial Crimes Enforcement Network, a part of the US Department of the Treasury, on FinCEN Form 114. The FBAR can be filed online using the Financial Crimes Enforcement Network's website.

Even though the FBAR is not filed with the IRS, the IRS has access to FinCEN records and references them when a taxpayer enrolls in certain IRS amnesty programs (More on this in Chapter 11). The taxpayer must also indicate on their tax return both that an FBAR was filed and which countries the taxpayer has accounts in.

For each of your accounts, you will need the following information for your FBAR filing:

- Account number, name, and address of the financial institution
- The maximum account value during the tax year (local currency should be converted to USD using the closing spot rate on December 31 of the tax year. This can be found on the Treasury website for all countries).
- Bureau of Fiscal Services currency exchange rate on the last day of the calendar year, to convert the local currency into USD
- If it is a joint account, the number of owners and principal joint owner's information.

The due date for FBAR filings is April 15, the same as for individual tax returns, although a six-month automatic extension is available.

If You Haven't Filed Even Though You Met The Threshold

Many expats are not aware of the obligation to file FBAR. If you didn't know about it and want to get back into compliance, the filing procedure can be quite simple. The IRS states that if you have been filing and paying your taxes on any income generated from these accounts and need only to file your delinquent FBARs, you can simply file the FBARs with the Treasury and provide a short statement as to why you did not file. If you are late on your taxes as well, the IRS offers programs to catch up on late filings without incurring penalties other than interest, provided you qualify for those programs. For more information about this, visit Chapter 11.

Furthermore, if you have specific foreign assets (financial assets, plus a few additional asset classes) that exceed certain IRS thresholds, there are additional filing requirements. You must report these assets to the IRS using form 8938 "Statement of Specified Foreign Financial Assets". This is a separate filing that is not part of your FBAR report and thresholds for this requirement are much higher than FBAR filing thresholds.

Form 8938 For Other Specified Foreign Financial Assets

During your time abroad, it's likely that you will accumulate a few assets, potentially including a few foreign financial assets that need to be reported on Form 8938, Statement of Specified Foreign Financial Assets. This form is for reporting foreign mutual funds, pensions, stocks, bonds, loans, and other foreign investments and accounts. Unlike the FBAR, Form 8938 is submitted to the IRS with your tax return. This gives it the same due date as your tax return.

The penalty for failure to file is up to $10,000. Plus, if you fail to file after the IRS notifies you, then you could be fined up to an additional $10,000 for every 30 days of non-filing, with a maximum potential penalty of $50,000. Furthermore, criminal penalties may also apply.

Who Needs To File Form 8938?

You are required to file Form 8938, if:

- You have specified foreign financial assets, and
- The value of your foreign financial assets exceeds the threshold.
- Let's explain what this means for you.

You Have Specified Foreign Financial Assets

This essentially means that you have one or more of the assets that are reported on this form. Briefly, a specified foreign financial asset is any financial account held at a foreign financial institution or some foreign investments that are not held in an account, for example, ownership of a foreign entity.

This means if you have any of the following, you might need to file Form 8938:

- Bank accounts
- Brokerage accounts
- Other financial accounts (deposit or custodial) that are held at a foreign financial institution
- Stock or securities issued by someone who is not a US person
- Foreign pensions
- Mutual funds
- Financial instruments or contracts with an issuer or counterparty who is not a US person
- Shares of foreign companies held through a non-US broker
- Any ownership in foreign entities, such as partnerships
- Foreign issued life insurance or annuity contract with a cash-value
- Foreign hedge funds and foreign private equity funds
- Foreign accounts and foreign non-account investment assets held by foreign or domestic grantor trust for which you are the grantor

- Any financial accounts (deposit or custodial) that are held at a foreign financial institution

In addition, if your foreign financial assets generated income, you need to include a summary of that income on your tax return. Certain physical assets such as gold bars, antiques, jewelry, and some other assets do not need to be reported.

While this may sound the same as the FBAR, the two filings are different, namely the due date, types of accounts that must be reported, and to whom the form is submitted.

Keep in mind that you only need to report assets once in your tax return. If you reported your foreign corporation on Form 5471, or a foreign trust on Form 3520, or a PFIC on Form 8621 then you do not need to report it again on Form 8938. The FBAR is completely separate though and must include all accounts. (More on PFICs in Chapter 10).

The Value Of Your Foreign Financial Assets Exceeds The Threshold.

Form 8938 has a higher threshold than the FBAR. Depending on how you and your spouse (if applicable) file taxes, where you reside, and the value of your assets, the threshold varies.

For a US person living outside of the US and filing as single or married filing separately,

Form 8938 is required if the value of the foreign assets exceeds:

- $200,000 on the last day of the tax year, or
- $300,000 at any time during the year.

A US person living abroad and filing a joint return must file Form 8938 if the value of the foreign assets exceeds:

- $400,000 on the last day of the tax year, or
- $600,000 at any time during the year.

These thresholds are for 2021 and may change in the future. The Form 8938 thresholds are not indexed for inflation.

The filing thresholds for Form 8938 are significantly lower for someone who lives in the United States. For a US person living in the United States and filing as single or married filing separately, Form 8938 is required if the value of the foreign assets exceeds:

- $50,000 on the last day of the tax year, or
- $75,000 at any time during the year.

A US person living in the United States and filing as single or married filing separately, Form 8938 is required if the value of the foreign assets exceeds:

- $100,000 on the last day of the tax year, or
- $150,000 at any time during the year.

Foreign Assets That Don't Need To Be Reported

Certain foreign assets do not need to be reported. Generally, these assets are of physical nature. US taxpayers do not need report:

- Physical gold and precious metals
- Safety deposit boxes at foreign banks and vaults
- Art
- Cars
- Antiques
- Jewelry
- Other collectibles
- Real estate held in your own name

While most of these assets are self-explanatory and straightforward, real estate, safety deposit boxes, and precious metals like gold and silver have unexpected nuances for reporting requirements.

Real Estate

Regardless of whether your real estate is foreign or domestic, it does not need to be reported to the US as long as it is held in your name. If the real estate is held in a foreign entity, then it may be a financial asset and reportable on Form 8938 or Form 5471. However, even when filing Form 8938 the real estate itself is not reported. Instead, the value of the property adds to the value of the entity and the entity is what is reported on the form. Keep in mind that any income, such as rental income, from your property still needs to be included on your tax return,

Furthermore, if you are married to an NRA spouse, then you do not need to report any assets held solely in the spouse's name as long as you don't elect to file jointly with them on a tax return. Chapter 9 has more information on filing jointly.

Safety Deposit Boxes

If you have a key to a safety deposit box and you are the only one who can access it, you don't have to report it. Safety deposit boxes are not considered foreign accounts and you can use them to store physical foreign currency, gold, and precious metals.

A safety deposit box only needs to be reported if there is a custodian involved. Even if you hold the key, many safety deposit boxes have custodians who can access the contents on your behalf, which would be reportable.

Gold And Silver

Only physical gold and silver, that you own outright, are exempt from reporting. Gold or silver bars, coins, or bullions do not need to be reported as long as you are the owner.

As with real estate, if your physical gold or silver is held by an entity then it is included when calculating the value of the entity.

If you own "paper" gold or silver, such as ETFs or stocks, through a brokerage account then you need to report it on the FBAR and Form 8938 (if you meet the thresholds). Any gold or silver that is pooled and gold held through a platform such as GoldMoney are reported on the same forms.

Chapter 8: US State Tax Considerations For Expats

You might think that moving away from the United States means that you are done with state taxes. However, that is not always the case. Some states continue to tax expats even after their move abroad.

We categorize states in three ways: friendly, neutral, or sticky.

Easy Vs. Difficult States For Expats

Generally, US states fall into three broad categories when it comes to expat state taxes: the easy ones, the somewhat neutral ones, and the difficult or "sticky" ones.

Easy States

These are states that don't have an individual income tax. Alaska, Florida, Nevada, South Dakota, Texas, Washington, and Wyoming all fall into this category. Tennessee and New Hampshire tax interest and dividends, but do not apply income taxes to wages and salaries. Several of these states also offer other tax incentives. Residents may receive reduced corporate taxes, property taxes, or inheritance taxes.

Neutral States

Most states are somewhere in between easy and difficult. These states will typically stop considering you a tax resident after you have been gone for a while. In some cases, you may have to prove your new place of residency and submit some paperwork, but you are unlikely to face any hurdles.

Difficult States

Virginia, California, New Mexico, and South Carolina are known for being difficult or "sticky" states. We have also seen issues with expats from Massachusetts, Maryland, and North Carolina. These states are known for going after former residents.

Some states assume that you will return to the state after living abroad and therefore should remain a tax resident for the entire time spent overseas. If you end up returning to your old home state after a few years abroad and start filing tax returns again, the state may notice the gap in filings. If you cannot prove that you were resident elsewhere during that time, they may require you to pay back taxes for the years spent abroad.

Residents of California need to be especially careful. California is one of the toughest states for Americans abroad when it comes to tax. Not only do you have to pay state tax on your income, but California does not allow for the Foreign Earned Income Exclusion. If you claim the FEIE on your federal income taxes, California will add it back in. This can also happen with other federal deductions such as the deduction for health savings accounts.

On the other hand, California does have a Safe Harbor Rule. This allows Californians with employment contracts abroad to be classified as non-residents for tax purposes. To qualify, the employment contract must be uninterrupted for at least 546 consecutive days (1.5 years) and the number of days you can spend in California are limited. In addition, if you earn investment income of over $200,000 during any of the years you are abroad, then you are ineligible for the Safe Harbor Rule.

If a tax document arrives at the address in the previous state, it may be flagged, and the state could be notified. This may trigger the state to send a letter to the taxpayer about owing tax. When possible, taxpayers should make these changes in writing for their records.

Move States To Save Tax

To avoid issues with your US state, especially if it is a sticky state, you need to show that you have no intentions of returning and move your residency to a new state. Taxpayers need to sever as many ties to the state as possible and create new ties in the new state. The tax authorities may consider additional factors.

One of the first things you should consider when moving states is your real estate in your current home state. We recommend that you sell your home in the previous state and purchase or lease a home in the new state. If you do not sell your home, do not treat it as your primary residence. Consider renting it out. In addition, be sure to update your homeowners' insurance policies so that your new home is listed as your primary residence. Once you have your home in the new state, use this as your address at all times. This means you will need to change your address anywhere it is registered. All mail needs to be received at the new address. Update your address to the new state with all of the following: banks and brokerage firms, credit card issuers, IRA custodians, Social Security, attorneys, insurance companies, magazines or newspapers you subscribe to, and professional or social organizations.

Close any local bank accounts from the previous state and open new ones in the previous state. Likewise, close or transfer any local brokerage accounts in the previous state. Make sure checks and statements show and are sent to your new address. Save them or make copies during the first year of your residence. If you receive Social Security benefits, have it deposited into an account in the new state. Rent a safety deposit box in the new state and end the lease on any safe deposit boxes in the previous state.

You should also register to vote in the new state and obtain a driver's license. Make sure to surrender your previous license. Keep expired licenses or make copies of them as proof of the original issue date. Other paperwork should also be transferred to or updated in the new state. Register all automobiles, boats, and airplanes in the new state. Save the registrations or a copy of them. You will also need to execute a will in the new state. Save a copy of the new will and a copy of your last will from the previous state. If available, file a declaration of domicile in the new state as well. Remember to file a final tax return in the previous state too.

In addition, your personal and family life should be connected to the new state. Join the local library, social groups, clubs, and recreational sports teams. If you are religious, become a member of the local church, temple, or other religious organization. You should resign from positions or memberships in the previous state. Moving any sentimental or valuable items to the new state, for example, heirlooms, photographs, collections, jewelry, artwork, antiques, or silver is another important step. Any insurance for valuable items should be associated with your new address. If you have any pets, they should live at your home in the new state.

Have your medical records forwarded to new providers, such as doctors and dentists, in the new state. If you have a pet, retain the services of a vet in the new state.

Professionals licensed in the previous state need to notify the issuing authority that they are leaving the state. If they plan to practice in the new state, they should obtain a license there. If you filed a certificate of doing business or a partnership certificate in the previous, request a change of address. The services of other professionals, such as lawyers or accountants, should be retained in the new state.

Finally, keep detailed records of the move and your life in the new state. Make as many of the changes as possible in writing. Keep originals or copies of any documentation associated with the above list. These records can be crucial in the case of an audit. For more about records expats should keep, visit Chapter 17.

However, the above list is extensive, and in some cases, it may be excessive. Depending on the situation it may not be necessary to take all of these steps. Rather, it should be assessed on an individual basis.

As always, when making significant financial or tax decisions, it is important to speak with an expert. Each situation is unique, and there are no one-size-fits-all solutions. Professional advice helps ensure that the domicile is correctly changed and reduces the likelihood of an audit or other issues.

Chapter 9: Married & Children Abroad

Some people move abroad with a spouse. Others move abroad for love or find love while overseas. Either way, your spouse may impact your US tax filing. This is especially true for Americans with a spouse who does not have US citizenship or a Green Card. Generally, married couples must either file jointly or file separately, though some may qualify to file as Head of Household.

Married To A US Person

Choosing the best tax filing status can be confusing, and which is most beneficial is not always clear. If you and your spouse are both US persons, you will need to run the numbers filing as Married Filing Jointly and as Married Filing Separately to see which is optimal.

Usually, filing your taxes with a spouse who has US citizenship or a Green Card is simpler than filing with a spouse who isn't a US person. Because you're both already US persons, you both have to file anyway. This means it's usually just a matter of checking both filing statuses to see which will save you the most money.

Married Filing Jointly With A US spouse

To file as Married Filing Jointly, a couple needs to agree to file jointly and to have been married as of December 31 of that tax year. If both spouses are US citizens or Green Card holders who are living abroad, they don't need to take any extra steps to file jointly.

Married Filing Separately With A US spouse

To qualify for Married Filing Separately, you need to be married as of December 31 of the tax year. This filing status can be a good choice for couples without children if one person is in a much higher tax bracket than the other and the other has high deductions. It can keep you and your spouse in a lower tax bracket than if you filed jointly and combined your income. However, if you file as Married Filing Separately you aren't eligible for certain tax breaks such as the Child Care Credit. As a strategy, we have seen couple divorce at the end of the year and remarry at the beginning of the year. Although we do not recommend this strategy due to its aggressive nature, it can be beneficial to file as single if both spouses are US people and high-income earners.

US Person Married To A Non-Resident Alien

If you are a US expat married to a nonresident alien, someone with neither US citizenship nor a Green Card, deciding how to file is a big decision. The election to include your foreign spouse in your tax return can only be made once, and it can only be revoked one time. Consequently, the tax impact of this decision is long-lasting and not to be taken lightly.

Here are a few key factors to keep in mind:

Tax Impact Of Married Filing Separately With A Foreign Spouse

The primary benefit of Married Filing Separately is that the NRA spouse does not need to file anything. Just the US citizen spouse must file, based on their own income.

By filing separately, your NRA spouse's income and assets are protected from US taxation and reporting. This is especially important if your NRA spouse has a high income or high-value investments. If you included them in your filing, it would likely significantly increase your tax liability.

You can shelter up to $159,000 (2021) of your assets from reporting (on the FBAR or Form 8939) and from US taxation on the income from these assets by gifting them to your non-resident foreign spouse on an annual basis. Of course, gifting significant assets only to avoid taxes and disclosure requires a substantial amount of trust in your spouse.

Usually, if you earn under the FEIE limit or if your Foreign Tax Credits offset most or all of your US taxes, then you and your spouse should file separately. Because your US tax bill is already at zero, you won't benefit from filing jointly.

In general, filing separately with an NRA spouse helps you and your spouse avoid the headache of requesting an Individual Taxpayer Identification Number (ITIN), filing US taxes, and having the NRA spouse on the IRS's radar.

Tax Impact Of Married Filing Jointly With A Foreign Spouse

If you file as Married Filing Jointly with an NRA spouse, you are creating a filing obligation for your spouse. Your spouse will be taxed on their worldwide income, just as if they were a US resident. This means all of their income will be subject to US taxation and that they may have to file Form 8938. They do not have to file an FBAR (unless they have other ties to the United States, for example passing the Substantial Presence Test). For more about the Substantial Presence Test, visit Chapter 2.

If you are a US person with a non-working NRA spouse in a low tax country and you earn over the FEIE threshold, then filing jointly may help you reduce your taxes. While filing jointly can help lower your tax bill if your foreign spouse has little or no income, it is not a decision to take lightly. When you file jointly with an NRA spouse, your spouse will be treated as a US person for tax purposes. This has significant tax implications and, as mentioned, the decision to include your foreign spouse in your tax return can only be made once, and it can only be revoked one time.

If you decide to file jointly, your NRA spouse must obtain an Individual Taxpayer Identification Number (ITIN).

Requesting An ITIN For Your Spouse

Normally, with a US spouse you would include your and your spouse's social security numbers on the tax return. A non-US person does not have a social security number and therefore must request an Individual Taxpayer Identification Number (ITIN) instead.

To apply for an ITIN, the NRA spouse needs a certified copy of their passport. They can also use two other forms of identification in place of a passport. One of these IDs should prove their identity and the other should prove their foreign status.

The issuing government agency can certify a passport or ID copy. Alternatively, you can hire a Certifying Acceptance Agent, which is a service authorized by the IRS, to authorize the passport copy. You can also mail your passport directly to the IRS for verification and they should send it back to you. If you can avoid it, we generally don't recommend mailing your passport to the IRS.

Once your spouse has received their certified passport copy, they will file a Form W-7 with your joint tax return. The IRS will process Form W-7 with the tax return and issue your spouse's ITIN.

Deductions And Exclusions

When filing a joint return with your foreign spouse, you can be eligible for higher deductions and exclusions, depending on the combined income levels.

Especially when it comes to the Foreign Earned Income Exclusion, your filing status can make a big difference. If you file a tax return as Single, Head of Household, or Married Filing Separately, you can exclude up to $108,700 (2021) from your foreign income by claiming the Foreign Earned Income Exclusion. If you however opt for a Married Filing Jointly return, and you and your spouse work abroad and each meet the

FEIE eligibility requirements, you can exclude up to $108,700 (2021) each. Keep in mind that one spouse cannot use the unused portion of the other's exclusion amount.

Contributions To Tax-Deferred Accounts

If you don't include your foreign spouse in your tax filing, your spouse will not be recognized as a US taxpayer. Therefore, he or she will not be able to make contributions to any tax-deferred, US-based account (such as an IRA), nor will you be able to contribute on his or her behalf.

As you can see, there is a lot to take into account. While the above considerations are important, there are more nuances regarding the tax impact of your foreign spouse.

To find which way of filing is most optimal you or your accountant should evaluate several filing statuses. In some cases, you can significantly lower your tax bill by filing jointly with your spouse on your tax return. In other situations, Married Filing Separately or as Head of Household would save you more money.

Head Of Household With An NRA Spouse And Dependents

Even though the Head of Household status is often used by unmarried individuals, US persons who are married to non-resident aliens can actually file as Head of Household too. For some individuals, this filing status can represent huge savings.

A few years ago, a client of ours, let's call him David, was able to significantly reduce his tax bill by switching from Married Filing Separately to Head of Household. He was working at a multinational in the Netherlands, his spouse was a non-resident alien, and he had three children who were US citizens.

In the previous tax year, a Big Four accounting firm had filed his tax return. (The Big Four firms are Deloitte, PricewaterhouseCoopers [PwC], Ernst & Young [EY], and Klynveld Peat Marwick Goerdeler [KPMG]. These are the four largest accounting firms in the world).

When we reviewed David's tax return, our team discovered that his return had not been filed in the most advantageous way. The previous firm had filed his previous tax return with the election married and filing separately. Because David's wife was an NRA and his children passed the Citizenship or Residence Test as US citizens, he was eligible to file as Head of Household. This is a somewhat nuanced part of tax law and many accountants are not familiar with the exception. Our team was able to amend his previous tax return and the Netherlands executive received a $20,000 refund.

To file as Head of Household you need to provide more than half the cost of supporting a qualifying dependent and more than half the cost of their home. The dependent cannot earn more than $4,300 (2021) per year and they need to pass the Citizenship or Residence Test. In short, this test requires that the dependent is a citizen or resident of the US, Canada, or Mexico, though there are a few exceptions (more on this below). A qualifying dependent could be a:

- Fiancé, girlfriend, or boyfriend
- Grandparent
- Parent
- Mother-in-law or Father-in-law
- Stepparent
- Sibling
- Half-sibling
- Stepsiblings
- Child
- Stepchild
- Adopted child
- Grandchild
- And more.

A non-resident alien spouse is not eligible to be a dependent for the purposes of the Head of Household filing status.

Citizenship Or Residence Test For Dependents

Along with meeting a few other requirements, your dependent needs to pass the Citizenship or Residence Test for you to claim Head of Household. To pass this test, the dependent needs to be a citizen or resident of the US, Mexico, or Canada.

In some rare situations, you may be able to file as Head of Household even if your children fail the Citizenship or Residence Test because they are not US citizens or residents. This situation is somewhat uncommon because usually US citizenship is given to the children of Americans. This can happen if you adopt a child from a foreign country or if you adopt your stepchildren who are not US persons. We've also seen this happen to children of US citizens who left the United States during their childhood and did not return. It's somewhat complex, but essentially if you leave the US during your youth and do not return, your citizenship may not be passed to your children.

In both of these situations, you should still be able to claim your children as dependents and file as Head of Household by requesting ITINs for them. As note, if you have not legally adopted your stepchildren, then they do not qualify as dependents for the purposes of Head of Household.

Legally Married In Another Country

We've seen a few cases of individuals who were married filing as Single because they were married in a foreign country, not the US. This is not correct. If you were legally married in another country, the US generally recognizes the marriage as legal.

This means you need to file your US tax return as Married Filing Separately, Married Filing Jointly, or as Head of Household, not Single.

The Single filing status is for individuals who were unmarried on the last day of the year. This includes individuals who are single, were never married, and who were divorced or legally separated before December 31 of the tax year. Individuals who qualify to file as Single should check to see if they qualify as Head of Household which could result in more tax savings.

Credits For Children And Dependents

US taxpayers typically can claim credits for qualifying children and other dependents. When living abroad, those credits may only be available in certain circumstances.

Child Tax Credit

With the Child Tax Credit, you can reduce your tax bill by claiming up to $2,000 (2021) in credits for each eligible child. If your tax bill is already at zero, then you may be able to get a refund with the Child Tax Credit. You can receive a refund of up to $1,400 (2021) per child. (Easily receiving refunds and making tax payments is a good reason for maintaining a US bank account).

The exact amount you are eligible for depends on your income. If you are filing as Single, Head of Household, or Married Filing Separately and earn $200,000 or less during 2021, then you qualify for the full amount. If you are Married Filing Jointly and earn $400,000 or less in 2021, then you also can claim the full Child Tax Credit amount. After these limits, the Child Tax Credit is phased out.

Expats can claim the Child Tax Credit in certain situations. If you exclude all of your income with the Foreign Earned Income Exclusion, then you are generally not eligible for the Child Tax Credit. If you claim the FEIE (and the Foreign Housing Exclusion or Deduction, if eligible) and still have non-excluded income then the Child Tax Credit could further reduce your tax burden. When claiming the FEIE, you cannot receive a refund from the Child Tax Credit.

US taxpayers who claim the Foreign Tax Credit are eligible for the credit or refund. After claiming the Foreign Tax Credit, if you still have a tax liability, you can apply up to $2,000 (2021) per child to your tax bill. If you have eliminated your entire US tax bill with the Foreign Tax Credit, then you can claim the Child Tax Credit and receive a refund from the IRS.

We often see US taxpayers in Europe, Australia, Canada, Japan, and other countries with taxes at or above US rates take advantage of this.

You also need to make sure your child qualifies. For you to claim your child for the Child Tax Credit, they need to:

- Be 16 years old or younger at the end of the tax year
- Be your child, stepchild, adopted child, or foster child
- Pass the Citizen or Resident Test
- Live with you for more than half of the year (some exceptions are allowed)
- Not provide more than half of their own support during the year

Credits For Other Dependents

You can also claim someone as a dependent if they are a brother, sister, stepbrother, stepsister, or a descendant, such as a grandchild or a nephew. This is called the Other Dependents Credit. Similar to the Child Tax Credit, other dependents need to pass the Citizen or Resident Test. This credit is only available for $500 (2021) and is non-refundable.

Child And Dependent Care Credit

Many Americans in foreign countries use nannies, babysitters, or before- and after-school programs, and other childcare services. If both spouses have jobs, then the amount paid to child caretakers can qualify for a tax credit of up to $4,000 (2021). Known as the Child and Dependent Care Credit, it can be used for expenses relating to the caretaking of children under age 13 or adults who cannot take care of themselves and have lived with you for at least half of the year. We have seen many expats take this credit due to the availability of help, particularly in countries in Asia, South America and Africa. An ITIN for a foreign caretaker is not required to claim these payments, so we encourage all clients to take this credit if eligible. Most of the time, to claim this both parents must work and file jointly, not separately. If you have a legal separation order in place or if you and your spouse have lived apart for at least the last six months of the tax year, you can still claim this credit and claim Married Filing Separately.

Eligible expenses for this credit include costs such as:

- Daycare
- Babysitters, housekeepers, cooks, or maids who take care of your child
- Day camps and summer camps (overnight camps do not qualify)
- Before- and after-school programs
- Nurses and aides who provide care for a dependent who is disabled
- Nursery school or preschool

For 2021, this credit phases out at $438,000. Based on your income, the percentage of expenses that can be claimed will change. In 2021, a taxpayer with a gross income of up to $125,000 can claim 50% of the credit. When calculating the amount you can claim, you can include up to $8,000 of eligible expenses for one dependent, or up to $16,000 of eligible expenses for two or more dependents. Depending on your income, you will then claim a percentage of those expenses.

The Child and Dependent Care Credit is nonrefundable for taxpayers whose abode wasn't in the United States for more than half the year, which means you can use the credit to lower your tax bill, but you won't receive a refund from the IRS if your tax bill is already at zero.

Chapter 10: Investing And Retirement Planning When Abroad

Moving abroad can mean new opportunities for investing and retirement planning but it can also get complicated quickly. While some Americans overseas contribute to foreign pensions, many prefer to continue contributions to their US retirement accounts. Fortunately, with some planning, Americans abroad can often continue investing in their IRAs, 401(k)s, and other retirement accounts. Still, this is an area that requires extra caution. If not handled properly, it can get messy and expensive quickly.

US Retirement Plans

American workers often contribute to individual retirement accounts (IRAs) as a form of retirement planning. These IRA retirement plans offer tax advantages, either via traditional contributions or Roth contributions. While IRAs can be an excellent retirement plan, contributing to these accounts while abroad requires some extra effort.

IRAs

In a Traditional IRA, your money is contributed to the account tax-free if you are eligible to take the deduction and is taxed later in the future when it is withdrawn. This can be a good option for individuals who expect their tax rate to be lower in the future. You can contribute to a Traditional IRA regardless of your income. The amount you can deduct though will depend on whether you or your spouse is covered by a retirement plan at work, your filing status, and your income.

Frequently people contribute to their traditional IRAs and either cannot or choose not to take the deduction, which means that the contribution is taxed. For instance, you cannot take a deduction on your Traditional IRA contributions if you already contribute to a 401(k) plan at work. The earnings grow tax free and are only taxed when distributed. The amounts contributed will not be taxed upon distribution, because they were contributed with pre-tax dollars.

Below are the IRA deduction limits if you are not covered by a retirement plan at work:

Filing Status	Modified Adjusted Gross Income	Deduction Amount
Single or Head of Household	Any amount	A full deduction up to the amount of your contribution limit.
Married Filing Jointly or Separately with a spouse who is <u>not</u> covered by a plan at work.	Any amount	A full deduction up to the amount of your contribution limit.
Married Filing Jointly with a spouse who <u>is</u> covered by a plan at work	$198,000 or less (2021); $204,000 or less (2022)	A full deduction up to the amount of your contribution limit.
	Between $198,000 and $208,000 (2021); $204,000 and $214,000 (2022)	A partial deduction
	$208,000 or more (2021); $214,000 or more (2022)	No deduction
Married Filing Separately with a spouse who <u>is</u> covered by a plan at work	Less than $10,000	A partial deduction
	$10,000 or more	No deduction

If you are covered by a retirement plan at work, the deduction limits are as follows:

Filing Status	Modified Adjusted Gross Income	Deduction Amount
Single or Head of Household	$66,000 or less (2021); $68,000 or less (2022)	A full deduction up to the amount of your contribution limit.
	Between $66,000 and $76,000 (2021); $68,000 and $78,000 (2022)	A partial deduction
	$76,000 or more (2021); $78,000 or more (2022)	No deduction
Married Filing Jointly	$105,000 or less (2021); $109,000 or less (2022)	A full deduction up to the amount of your contribution limit.
	Between $105,000 and $125,000 (2021); $109,000	A partial deduction

	and $129,000 (2022)	
	$125,000 or more (2021); $129,000 or more (2022)	No deduction
Married Filing Separately	Less than $10,000	A partial deduction
	$10,000 or more	No deduction

Moreover, to contribute to a Traditional IRA while abroad expats need to have non-excluded earned income. If they exclude all their income under the FEIE (see Chapter 3), they cannot contribute. We'll explain more about this soon.

With a Roth IRA, you contribute with after tax dollars, and withdrawals in the future are tax-free. This can be advantageous for individuals who expect their tax rate to go up in the future. However, the amount you can contribute to a Roth IRA depends on your filing status and Modified Adjusted Gross Income. Your Modified Adjusted Gross Income is your income (and your spouse's) Adjusted Gross Income plus certain deductions and the FEIE and Foreign Housing Exclusion or Deduction added back. As an American abroad, your Modified Adjusted Gross Income is may be significantly higher than your Adjusted Gross Income, depending on if you take the FEIE or not.

Below are the filing thresholds for Roth IRAs 2021:

Filing Status	Modified Adjusted Gross Income	Contribution Limit
Single, Head of Household, or Married Filing Separately (and you did not live with your spouse at any time during the year)	Less than $125,000	Up to $6,000 (Up to $7,000 if you're 50 years old or over)
	Between $125,000 and $140,000	A reduced amount
	Over $140,000	$0
Married Filing Separately and you lived with your spouse at any time during the year	Less than $10,000	A reduced amount
	Over $10,000	$0
Married Filing Jointly or qualifying widow(er)	Less $198,000	Up to $6,000
Married Filing Jointly or qualifying widow(er)	Between $198,000 and $208,000	A reduced amount
	Over $208,000	$0

Below are the filing thresholds for Roth IRAs 2022:

Filing Status	Modified Adjusted Gross Income	Contribution Limit
Single, Head of Household, or Married Filing Separately (and you did not live with your spouse at any time during the year)	Less than $129,000	Up to $6,000 (Up to $7,000 if you're 50 years old or over)
	Between $129,000 and $144,000	A reduced amount
	Over $144,000	$0
Married Filing Jointly or qualifying widow(er)	Less $204,000	Up to $6,000
	Between $204,000 and $214,000	A reduced amount
	Over $214,000	$0

Similar to Traditional IRAs, Americans abroad can contribute to a Roth IRA as long as they have non-excluded income. This can be difficult for US taxpayers who exclude all of their income with the Foreign Earned Income Exclusion. Fortunately, you do have a few options. I'll explain these soon.

401(k) Plans

401(k) plans are company-sponsored retirement accounts. In these accounts, both employers and employees usually make contributions. Whether you have a Traditional 401(k) or a Roth 401(k) depends on when you will be taxed. Under a Traditional 401(k), income used for contributions is not taxed, but withdrawals during retirement are taxed. With a Roth 401(k), employees make contributions using after- tax earned income and their withdrawals are tax-free.

To contribute to a 401(k) plan, you need to be employed by a US company that offers one. If you are self-employed, you may be able to set up a Solo 401(k). (More on this soon). Generally speaking, if your US employer offers the option to contribute to a 401(k), you can continue to do so while abroad. Still, this is a nuanced part of tax law where it is worth seeking personalized, professional advice that considers where you are living and working, and your specific 401(k) plan.

If you are no longer able to contribute your company 401(k) after moving abroad, you may want to consider rolling over your 401(k) to an IRA.

Making Contributions With Non-Excluded Income

You cannot make a contribution to an IRA with income that is excluded from taxation. This can be an obstacle for Americans overseas who often exclude their income from income tax using the Foreign Earned Income Exclusion (Chapter 3) and the Foreign Housing Exclusion and Deduction (Chapter 4). This leaves them without non-excluded income to contribute to their IRA.

This can be remedied in a few different ways. First, if you have foreign income that exceeds the FEIE limit, then that income is non-excluded income and can be contributed. Second, income that is not foreign earned, for example from working during a business trip in the US, is not excluded and therefore can be used for IRA contributions. Third, if you claim the Foreign Tax Credit instead of the FEIE, then your income is not excluded and can be used for deposits into retirement accounts.

Despite this, you should keep in mind that some custodians of retirement accounts don't like it if you are in a foreign country or a treaty country and may cancel your account if they realize that you are outside of the US. In our experience, Interactive Brokers and Charles Schwab have been the most amicable to expats. We also recommend using a US address to avoid issues. More on this in Chapter 1.

Roth IRA Conversions

Perhaps you worked in the US for several years and have now moved abroad. You may have accumulated some sort of retirement savings when working at a US company (likely a 401(k), 403(b), or another qualified retirement plan). Or maybe you have a Traditional IRA. Regardless of whether the funds are in a Traditional 401(k) or a Traditional IRA, if you are using the Foreign Earned Income Exclusion, you may be able to convert a portion of those pre-tax funds each year to a Roth IRA for free. To qualify for this strategy, you must have:

- All or close to all of your income excluded by the Foreign Earned Income Exclusion (FEIE) and Housing Exclusion and
- If you have non-excluded income it must be less than your standard or itemized deductions

This means that if you earn a lot more than the FEIE maximum, you most likely will not qualify. Likewise, if you have a significant amount of investment income, interest, or rental income (greater than the standard deduction total of $12,550 for single filers, $25,100 for joint filers with no children in 2021) you may not be able to qualify unless you have significant other deductions.

If you do qualify, you can convert the amount of Traditional IRA or rollover 401(k) funds to a Roth IRA that is equal to or less than the unused deduction amount.

You can likewise use this strategy if you have no earned income and still have some deduction surplus, but the Alternative Minimum Tax (AMT) can come into play here, so be careful.

Roth IRA conversions must be done by the end of the calendar year. To plan how much pre-tax funds you can convert tax-free to Roth, you'll need to know before the calendar year-end with reasonable certainty how much income you will earn in each category. If you convert too much you generate a tax liability. If you convert too little, you leave money on the table. US taxpayers have a few things to consider before you do any conversions this year:

- Are you taking the Foreign Earned Income Exclusion or Foreign Tax Credit for your earned income? You likely can't use this strategy in conjunction with the Foreign Tax Credit (For more about the Foreign Tax Credit, visit Chapter 5).
- Can you exclude all of your earned income, or nearly all of it, with the Foreign Earned Income Exclusion?
- Will you have sufficient "surplus" deduction amounts to cover your conversion and make it worth the trouble?
- Do you already have a Roth IRA? If not, you can easily set one up before the conversion.

Note that if you made a portion of your aggregate Traditional IRA holdings using non-deductible contributions, it will affect the calculation. This is known as the IRA Aggregation Rule. Here, we assumed that all IRA contributions are pre-tax, either through a traditional deductible IRA, 401(k), or 403(b) plans.

Before doing a Roth IRA conversion, you should seek the guidance of an experienced tax advisor. While the benefits can be significant, converting incorrectly could end in an unexpected tax bill.

More Retirement Planning Options For Business Owners

Business owners have additional options for retirement planning, such as Solo 401(k)s, Self-Directed IRAs, SEP IRAs, and Defined Benefit Plans. These offer significantly higher contribution limits and expanded investment options.

Solo 401(k)

A Solo 401(k), also known as an individual 401(k) or self-employed 401(k) is a type of retirement plan. They have many advantages including the ability to choose how your funds are invested, to contribute more, and to reduce your tax burden. If you own a company without full-time employees other than yourself and your spouse, opening a Solo 401(k) may be a good option. To open a solo 401(k) as a US citizen living abroad, you must:

- Be self-employed or a business owner

- Earn income that was not excluded from US tax using the FEIE (Foreign Earned Income Exclusion) or the Foreign Housing Exclusion (S Corp and C Corp owners can potentially exclude their wages and contribute on the employer side as a business expense)
- Have no eligible employees

Non-resident aliens, part-time employees or employees who work less than 1,000 hours per year, and employees younger than 21 years old can all be considered ineligible. If your business has ineligible employees, contact a specialist when structuring your Solo 401(k) plan. It is crucial that the language in your plan clearly explains their ineligibility and that any local labor laws are followed.

One strategic advantage of Solo 401(k)s is the opportunity to contribute higher amounts to your plan than with a SEP IRA (more on these soon). Both SEP IRAs and 401(k)s have the same annual maximum contribution amount, but you can get there faster with a Solo 401(k) because you are able to do employee deferral, which is when money is taken out of your income and contributed to the retirement account before you receive it. As an employer, you can contribute 25% of the adjusted earned income.

You can contribute up to $58,000 (2021) and $61,000 (2022). If you are over the age of 50, the limit is higher. Individuals over 50 years of age can deposit up to $64,500 (2021) and $67,500 (2022).

As an employee, you can contribute up to $19,500 (2021) and $20,500 (2022). After 50 years of age, you can contribute up to $26,000 (2021) and $27,000 (2022) to your Solo 401(k). Then, as an employer, you can contribute again. The percentage you can contribute as the employer will vary depending on how your business is structured and net earnings.

With a Solo 401(k) you might be able to reduce your tax burden. When contributing to your Solo 401(k), you have a few options for how your contributions are taxed. If planned properly, the savings can be significant. Contributions made as an employer must be made pre-tax (Traditional) and will be taxed upon withdrawal during retirement. Employer contributions cannot be made after tax (Roth).

Your contributions as an employee can be either pre-tax or after-tax. If you expect your tax obligations to be less after retirement, then a pre-tax contribution is your best option. This is known as a Traditional plan. If you choose to make your Solo 401(k) contributions pre-tax (Traditional), you can deduct the contributions from your US taxable income. Once you begin making withdrawals from your Traditional Solo 401(k) after age 59 ½, the withdrawals will be taxed as ordinary income. The income taxes will be applied at your future rate.

If you expect your tax obligations to increase after retirement, then you will want to use an after-tax contribution (Roth). If you decide to make Roth contributions, the amount you contribute comes from your normal after-tax income. There will not be any deductions. However, once you begin making withdrawals after the age of 59 ½, the withdrawals will be tax-free.

Increases or decreases in tax rates, returns on large investments, working during retirement, or other life changes that will move you into a different tax bracket are important factors when deciding how to structure your retirement plan.

A Roth Solo 401(k) is a great option, and the only option, for those who would like to contribute to a Roth but make over the income limits [$140,000 (2021) and $144,000 (2022) filing as single and $208,000 (2021) and $214,000 (2022) filing as joint].

Self-Directed IRA

A Self-Directed IRA (SDIRA), also known as a checkbook IRA, is a retirement account that allows you to invest in any investment allowed by law. A self-directed IRA is the same as any other IRA, except that you control and chose the investments. This is possible because your Self-Directed IRA will be the owner of an LLC that you manage.

When setting up a Self-Directed IRA, you need to work with an IRS approved custodian. Once the Self-Directed IRA account is set up, you can fund the account with an initial contribution or by transferring funds from a different retirement account. You can roll over funds from your Traditional IRA, a Roth IRA, SEP IRA, 401(k), or any other retirement account. The contributions are still either Traditional or Roth, and contribution limits and rules are the same.

Next, a Limited Liability Company (LLC) will be created for the Self-Directed IRA. Without an LLC, a Self-Directed IRA does not leverage its full benefits and you must rely on the custodian to carry out your wishes.

Finally, you can now use your LLC to make investments in both traditional and alternative investment options, free from custodian consent. While the process can seem intimidating in terms of paperwork and structuring, the process usually only takes a few weeks. At our firm, Global Expat Advisors, we help you set up a Self-Directed IRA with a US or offshore LLC, and prepare all required tax filings. Here is a recap of the basic steps in the process:

1. Open a custodial account at brokerage house.
2. Once account is opened then transfer your IRA funds from the current custodian to your new Self-Directed IRA custodian.
3. Open an LLC and bank account for Self-Directed IRA investment purposes
4. Transfer money from Self-Directed IRA custodial account to your LLC bank account which will be your Self-Directed IRA investment vehicle

5. (Optional) Open foreign company and foreign bank account and transfer funds from the LLC to this offshore vehicle so all assets are titled in name of the foreign LLC.
6. Make investments with the LLC. Make sure that no assets are titled in your name and that you do not touch any of the IRA money nor contribute/deposit any personal money directly into the LLC bank accounts or receive any income in your name personally. If this happens, it will be considered a distribution and potentially blow up the IRA.

One of the primary benefits of a SDIRA is that it allows Americans abroad to invest in a variety of investments. The investment diversity of a Self-Directed IRA can be especially appealing to someone with foreign investments. You can direct your funds towards investments, such as:

- Single/multi-family rental property
- Commercial real estate
- Raw land
- Contractual interest in real estate
- Water rights
- Mineral rights, oil and gas
- Real estate development tax liens
- LLC membership interest in technology, manufacturing and other service businesses
- Limited Partnership interest ("LP") in the business of real estate, technology, manufacturing and other service businesses
- Corporation, C Corp, in technology, manufacturing and other service businesses
- Real estate loan, promissory note and deed of trust/mortgage
- Business loan, secured by equipment/assets of business
- Purchase of livestock
- Gold, silver, and other precious metals
- Hedge funds investments in private placement companies
- Intellectual property patent interest
- Private placement memorandum investments
- Stock options and warrants of non-publicly traded company ownership

Self-Directed IRAs also offer the opportunity to invest when no financing is available (i.e., foreign real estate) or it would be impossible to get exposure via a Traditional IRA custodian. However, the law excludes some investment types. Specifically, you cannot invest in collectibles like art or stamps, in life insurance, or an S Corporation stock. Furthermore, investments that involve transactions with close family members and self-dealing are disqualified. Both authors have used their Self-Directed IRA to invest in real estate in Colombia due to the lack of financing available there. Using their Self-Directed

IRA funds, a local entity (Colombian SAS) was opened, and the funds transferred there. Once the funds were in Colombia, the local entity purchased the investment property there. The property is used only for investments and rent is paid to the Self-Directed IRA bank account as well as all expenses directly related to the investment property (HOA fees, property taxes, etc.) service.

Offshore Self-Directed IRA

In an Offshore IRA, the SDIRA is a member and owner of a foreign LLC so you can make foreign investments easily and quickly. In some cases, individuals will have the Self-Directed IRA own a US LLC which owns a foreign LLC. This is not a tax advantage. Rather, offshore Self-Directed IRAs offer asset protection.

Another benefit of having your Self-Directed IRA as the owner of an LLC is to maintain control. Normally, the SDIRA is overseen by an investment advisor, who is directed by you and carries out your wishes. More accurately though, the advisor takes your investment requests under consideration, but you cannot force him to execute instructions he is not comfortable with. That means you do not directly control the assets of the IRA.

To maintain control, you can open an LLC, either in the US or offshore, which will own the IRA and serves as an investment vehicle for the self-directed IRA. With this change, you as the LLC manager control the assets. While an offshore LLC offers the advantage of asset protection, it comes with increased costs and hassle as it requires both local and US filings.

Backdoor Roth IRAs

A backdoor Roth IRA actually isn't a type of retirement account. Rather, it's a strategy to contribute funds to a Roth IRA even if you exceed the income limit and contribute more than the contribution limits. In short, it's a legal way to contribute to a Roth IRA even if you have a high income.

With a backdoor IRA, you can convert your traditional IRAs or 401(k)s into a Roth IRA.

As you may recall from the previous section, a Roth IRA is a type of retirement account where you pay taxes on the income when you contribute it, and then, at retirement, the income is tax-free.

Unfortunately, the amount you can contribute to a Roth IRA is phased out at a certain income level. Then finally, once you have a modified adjusted gross income of $140,000 (2021) and $144,000 (2022) filing Single or $208,000 (2021) and $214,000 (2022) as Married Filing Jointly, you can't contribute at all.

A backdoor IRA is one way to overcome this. It works by rolling over a Traditional IRA (which has no income limit) or 401(k) plan into a Roth IRA. If it's an existing 401(k) or Traditional IRA, you can rollover as much as you want, even if it's more than the annual contribution limit for Roth IRAs. This means that you can even roll over your entire Traditional IRA or 401(k) at one time if you want.

You should keep a few things in mind before doing a backdoor Roth IRA. First, you still will owe taxes on any money rolled over from the Traditional IRA that hasn't already been taxed. This includes taxes on the initial contribution and on any income it has earned during the time you had it invested. Second, the taxable converted funds will be considered ordinary income, which could bump you into a higher tax bracket when you file taxes. Third, the funds you convert won't be accessible penalty-free for five years. And finally, if you have a mix of both deductible and non-deductible contributions in your Traditional IRA account, you will be forced to convert a pro-rata portion of the deductible funds when making any sort of conversion. Despite these considerations, a backdoor Roth IRA is still a powerful tool for investors. A backdoor IRA still lets you overcome Roth IRA contribution and income limits. This is a huge benefit for those who aren't able to contribute usually.

At Online Taxman, we help our clients with this analysis and ensure they are in compliance with this complex procedure.

Simplified Employee Pension (SEP) IRA

Simplified Employee Pension (SEP) IRAs are also popular retirement accounts that are usually set up by an employer for their employees. They can be set up by self-employed individuals as well. With a SEP IRA, only the employer can make contributions. The maximum SEP IRA contribution for is $58,000 (2021) and $61,000 (2022).

SEP IRAs can be a good option if your income surpasses the FEIE threshold because your contributions to a SEP IRA reduce your taxable income, the same way a 401(k) does.

The advantage of a SEPs is that they can be set up until the date you file your taxes, whereas 401(k)s must be set up by year end. If you're employed by your S Corp, you have to make your employee contributions by December 31 for the 401(k). In situations like this, a SEP IRA can offer a little extra time to make contributions.

LLCs and Sole Proprietorships do not require that you make employee contributions before December 31 for 401(k)s, because they don't have a fixed salary. But you're still supposed to mark the funds and make plans for the investment by December 31 of that tax year.

Defined Benefit Plans

Americans abroad should also consider a Defined Benefit Plan. This allows sole owner entrepreneurs to put away hundreds of thousands of dollars to a pension account, depending on their income, age, and the performance of their investment portfolio. However, they usually only make sense for individuals age 50 or older. This is because at age 50 you have a shorter contribution period until retirement and therefore can contribute much higher amounts annually. A longer period would mean low contribution amounts over a long period of time.

Unlike 401(k)s and some of the other plans discussed here, Defined Benefit Plans are typically only funded by the employer. However, if you are a self-employed individual or business owner, this won't impact you much as you have the ability to contribute as an employer. Usually, an advisor is hired to help with the management of the plan's investments and risk.

A Defined Benefit Plan is a type of employer-sponsored retirement plan. After retirement, the employee usually will receive benefits as a lifetime annuity or sometimes as lump-sum, depending on the plan's rules. Under a lifetime annuity, you receive payments from the plan until your death. In many cases, a spouse may be entitled to benefits if the beneficiary passes away.

Foreign Social Security

Many Americans who live and work abroad are enrolled in foreign social security systems. Expats are often required to enroll in another country's social security system if they are employed or self-employed resident of the country. Whether you have to contribute to a foreign social security system and how it will be taxed depends on that country's laws and whether the US has a tax treaty or totalization agreement with the country.

For example, US taxpayers in Spain need to check the totalization agreement between the United States and Spain to determine where their social security payments will go. In other cases, the country may not have a tax treaty or totalization agreement with the US. For instance, the US and Hong Kong have not signed a tax treaty or a totalization agreement. This means that US expats working in Hong Kong could potentially owe social security taxes in two countries. Fortunately, Hong Kong will allow you to opt-out of contributing to their retirement fund, the Mandatory Provident Fund as long as you are participating in a foreign retirement scheme.

In other countries, including Singapore and Costa Rica, you may be required to contribute to their national social security plans even if you would prefer to contribute to US Social Security. When this is the case, you can claim a Foreign Tax Credit at the end of the year for taxes paid to a foreign social security plan. For more information about the Foreign Tax Credit, go to Chapter 5.

Some Americans abroad want to contribute to a foreign social security system. This may be because the social security tax rate in the foreign country is lower or because they plan to withdraw from the foreign social security system during retirement.

If you have the option to choose which plan to pay into, consider how long you have been contributing to US Social Security. Taxpayers are only eligible for withdrawals from US Social Security after 40 quarters (essentially 10 years) of contributions. If you have already contributed for several years, it may be worth it to continue contributing until you meet the 40-quarter threshold. Usually, you will not have a choice as which plan to pay into as it is often dictated by tax treaties, social security totalization agreements, and a country's law.

Whether you even have the option to contribute to a foreign social security system or not, depends on where you live and what the totalization agreement says (if they have one). Read more about this in the Chapter 6 on tax treaties.

Taxation Of Retirement Distributions

Americans who retire abroad and receive US Social Security or make withdrawals from their retirement account (such as a Traditional IRA), may need to pay taxes on that income. The IRS does not consider US Social Security earned income. This means that you cannot claim the Foreign Earned Income Exclusion on it. US Social Security payments that are over a certain threshold are taxable. If your total income is more than $25,000 for an individual or $32,000 as Married Filing Jointly, you must pay income taxes on your Social Security benefits. Below those thresholds, your benefits are not taxed.

Whether distributions from a foreign retirement plan will be taxed by the US, by the country you live in, or the country in which the pension is based, depends on a multitude of factors, including whether the countries share a tax treaty. Planning and preparing for your retirement is one of the most important financial decisions you can make. Choices for how you prepare and how much you invest can have a significant impact on your future.

Taxation Of Foreign Pensions In The US

When contributing to a foreign pension, keep in mind that they are frequently viewed by the IRS as taxable investment accounts. Furthermore, unlike IRAs and 401(k)s, they are not usually tax-favored except in a few select countries, such as the United Kingdom. This means that foreign pensions do not receive the tax benefits, such as tax-free contributions or growth, of IRAs and 401(k)s. You may get a tax deduction or tax exemption in another country, but in the US foreign pension income is are usually treated as income in the year that it occurred. Fortunately, in tax treaty countries, the withdrawals are usually tax free or at least only taxed by the country of residence.

Instead, both employer contributions and growth in a foreign pension increase your taxable income and can be taxed by the US government. In other words, once your foreign pension is included in your tax return, your tax bill may be higher than you expected. The US could also potentially tax you twice on the same income, once on the accrued value of the account which is considered income, and a second time when you receive distributions from the account, if you do not carefully track the basis in the account.

The basis of the account are the employer contributions and growth in the account. Basis does not get taxed when it is withdrawn. Because of this, it's extremely important that people with foreign pensions keep track of their basis from year to year to avoid being taxed twice on their foreign pension. If it's properly tracked, there should not be double taxation by the US. Still, it's possible that it could potentially be taxed by a foreign country.

You may also face taxation from the country the pension is in or in your country of residence. Ultimately though, what will be taxed and how much you will owe usually comes down to a tax treaty. (If you are not familiar with tax treaties be sure to read Chapter 6).

If your foreign pension plan is held with an employer, a private plan, or an old prior employer plan, other factors could come into play. Likewise, if the plan is discriminatory or if your income is high, it could be taxed differently. Another issue is that foreign pension plans that invest in foreign mutual funds or exchange-traded funds (ETFs) may be classified as a passive foreign investment company (PFIC). Whether a pension plan is exempt from this reporting depends. If income from a pension is covered by a tax treaty (for example in the United Kingdom or Belgium), then it would not be required to report. However, sometimes people set up "retirement plans" (such as the insurance mentioned later in this chapter) that are not really pension plans in the eyes of the IRS or treaties and they invest in PFICs, thus causing a reporting obligation.

Finally, remember that your foreign pension account will likely need to be reported on the Foreign Bank Account Report (FBAR), Form 8938, and potentially on Form 8621 if it is a PFIC.

This is a very complex area of international tax law where variations in types of foreign pensions, tax treaties, your income, and more all play a role. Consider consulting a tax expert both in the US and in the country of the pension.

The Risk Of Foreign Investments, Life Insurances, And Pension Plans To Be Taxed As PFIC

The biggest negative tax impact occurs if a foreign investment turns out to be a PFIC (Passive Foreign Investment Company). PFICs are subject to punitive and complex tax rules, which aim to discourage US taxpayers from passive investments abroad. US expats need to be aware of and avoid PFICs if possible. The IRS defines a PFIC as a foreign corporation with:

- either at least 75% of the corporation's gross income is passive income,
- or at least 50% of the corporation's assets are passive assets

Most people assume that they don't own any PFICs. However, investments outside the US such as mutual funds, even money market funds, insurance policies, and non-US pension plans typically pool foreign investments and they meet the definition of a PFIC. One PFIC trap we often see is foreign life insurance.

As a US expat working abroad, you may have been offered a foreign life insurance policy. While this may sound like a good idea, it can be fraught with unintended US tax consequences. Rarely does the foreign life insurance policy meet the strict definition of the IRS for life insurances. Therefore, you won't enjoy the preferential tax treatment of life insurance. Instead, the IRS considers it a foreign financial investment, which can cause various tax and reporting consequences, including Form 8938. You may also be required to pay a quarterly excise tax on the value of the premiums.

For example, many financial advisors might try to sell a Malta fund with a life insurance wrapper. Some claim that it is supported by the US Malta tax treaty, however this does not apply to all pension plans and life insurance policies coming out of Malta. We would advise to be skeptical of these types of investments due to the fact that there may not be economic substance in the country to justify a tax treaty claim. In other words, if you're not a resident in the country and don't have any ties there, you likely will not be able to utilize the tax treaty.

If your foreign life insurance does not meet the IRS definition for life insurance and is instead a PFIC, you will have to report all the mutual funds held in the investment on Form 8621. Furthermore, when you die the PFICs inside the policy may be treated as sold and trigger tax as well, subject to excess distribution depending on how the pension is set up. As you can see, PFIC taxation is extremely complex.

With a life insurance, your goal is to provide assistance to your beneficiaries in the case of your death. However, if the insurance policy does not meet the IRS definition, it will be treated just like any other investment account. As such it is part of the assets that are subject to estate tax. This area of taxation of foreign investment products, pensions, tax treaties is very complicated, and we recommend speaking to a tax advisor for personalized advice.

Real Estate In The US And Abroad

Real estate is often one of the largest investments we make during our lives. Regardless of whether you only maintain a residence for yourself or you own rental properties, your foreign and US real estate can have a substantial impact on your tax return.

Home Sale Exclusion

Homeowners can potentially exclude several hundred thousand dollars when selling their home. Individuals Married Filing Jointly can exclude up to $500,000. (For more on Married Filing Jointly, visit Chapter 9). All other filing statuses can exclude up to $250,000 in capital gains. You can use this exclusion for your home in the US or a home in a foreign country. Generally speaking, you can only use the Home Sale Exclusion once every two years. To qualify, you must pass the ownership test and the personal use test.

The ownership test requires that you have owned the home for at least two of the last five years.

To meet the personal use test, you must have lived in or used the home as your primary residence for at least two of the last five years. If you have a spouse, you must both treat it as your primary residence or the amount you are eligible for may be reduced.

In some cases, you may be able to claim the Home Sale Exclusion even if you don't pass the personal use test, for example if you lived in or owned the home for less than two years, moved more than 50 miles away for new employment, for certain medical reasons, and in some other specific situations. In this case, only a partial exclusion can be claimed.

While the Home Sale Exclusion is impactful, many expats who move abroad and decide to keep their home in the US and rent it out. This can affect their eligibility for the exclusion. If you decide to sell the property after renting it out, you may completely lose the ability to claim Home Sale Exclusion or only be able to claim a partial exclusion.

However, if before moving from your primary residence, you sell your property to an S Corp that you own, you can claim the Home Sale Exclusion and exclude either $250,000 (Single) or $500,000 (Married Filing Jointly). To do this, you need a bona fide sale, an actual appraisal, and to sell the property at fair market value. For the transaction to be a bona fide sale, you need to have at least 10% to 20% of the sale amount in cash in the S Corp so that the S Corp can pay you for the property. From there, the S Corp can pay you over time. This is called an Installment Sale.

The sale to the S Corp also gives the property a step up in basis. This means that if you decide to sell the property later on, you will be depreciating the fair market value at sale to the S Corp and not the cost you paid when you originally bought the property. While this may seem somewhat complex, it really just means that if you sell the property later the initial exclusion amount of up to $250,000 or $500,000 from when you sold the property to the S Corp will remain free from capital gains tax and you will be able to take a higher depreciation deduction.

Now, executing this strategy can be somewhat complex as you will need to open an S Corp, make elections about how the payment will be treated, attribute the income from the sale correctly, ensure that the sale is bona fide, and more.

Rental Properties And Vacation Homes

Many expats are hesitant to sell their home when they move abroad. They may prefer to rent it out while they're overseas. Other Americans see investing in US or foreign rental properties as an exciting opportunity, regardless of where they live.

The rules for leasing a property can get complex fairly quickly and your property will be taxed differently depending on how you use it. If you rent out your vacation home for 14 or less days in the year, then your rental income is tax-free. Moreover, that income does not need to be reported, though this means that any expenses associated with renting the property won't be deducted either. However, if you rent out your second home for more than 14 days, then the income is taxable and must be reported as income on your tax return. Since you are reporting this income, you will be able to deduct your rental expenses.

How much you can deduct changes, based on whether the IRS considers the rental a business or personal residence. Your rental is a business if you personally used the property for 14 days or fewer, or for less than 10% of the days it was rented. As a rental business, you can deduct all eligible expenses associated with the property, plus any losses up to $25,000, depending on your income. You must report your rental property (in the US or abroad), along with the income earned, days it was rented out, and the days of personal use.

Reporting Requirements For Foreign Real Estate

Ownership of foreign real estate in itself does not need to be reported to the US government. As mentioned in Chapter 7, this is an asset type that does not come with reporting obligations. However, if like many investors or as is common in many countries, you choose to own your foreign real estate through a US or foreign entity, then you may incur some reporting obligations because foreign entities that own real estate frequently need to be reported on Form 5471 (more on this in Chapter 12) or Form 8858.

Of course, you must still report the rental income and when you sell a rental property, the loss or gain on the property is reported in your tax return, regardless of whether it is held in a foreign entity or not. A loss is not reported for a primary residence.

1031 Exchanges Of Real Estate

1031 exchanges can be a great strategy for investors in US or foreign property. Also known as a like-kind exchange, this allows investors to defer capital gains taxes by swapping one investment property for another. Usually, a swap is a taxable event. But with a 1031 exchange, little or no taxes are due at the time of the exchange. Instead, the capital gains tax can be deferred.

The IRS does not limit how many times you can do a 1031 exchange or how frequently. This means you can roll over the gain on one property into a new property, an unlimited number of times, potentially deferring your capital gains taxes for years. This is possible even if you profit on each swap. If done correctly, you'll only pay one tax at the end at a long-term capital gains rate which is usually lower than a short-term rate.

1031 exchanges are usually done with business or investment properties. You can also do a 1031 exchange with former residences and vacation homes though it is more difficult and extra requirements apply. Regardless, in order to make the swap the properties must be considered like-kind by the IRS. Fortunately, like-kind is actually more flexible than you would initially think. For example, you could exchange a city apartment for a ranch, or a home in the suburbs for a beach condo. You cannot exchange US property for foreign property, or vice versa. But you can do a 1031 between different foreign countries (for example, sell your beachfront rental property in Bocas del Toro, Panama for a finca ranch in the mountains of Medellin, Colombia). Primary residences are generally not eligible for 1031 exchanges unless they become a rental property after.

1031 exchanges can get complex. You must follow special rules for vacation homes, former residences, and depreciable property, or you could lose out on the benefits.

1031 exchanges are limited to real estate which changed in the 2017 Trump Tax plan. You cannot swap corporate stocks or partnership interests or cryptocurrency with a 1031 exchange.

Taxation Of Cryptocurrencies

In the last few years, the IRS has begun increasing their focus on cryptocurrency. In fact, in July of 2019, the IRS sent over 10,000 letters to taxpayers notifying them that they might have a reporting obligation. The IRS sent letters to individuals who may have incorrectly reported, underreported, or who did not report cryptocurrency at all. Taxpayers who did not report could incur taxes, penalties, interest, or even criminal prosecution. Another recent sign of the IRS's growing focus on cryptocurrency was in 2019, when they added a new question about cryptocurrency on Form 1040. In 2020, the form was updated to ask, "At any time during 2020, did you receive, sell, send, exchange, or otherwise acquire any financial interest in any virtual currency?" In 2019, the IRS also released much-needed guidance on the tax treatment of virtual currencies and accounting methods.

Accounting Methods

Any time you sell crypto at an exchange, to another person, or buy goods or services, it is a tax event for the US (and many other countries). In the IRS's view, digital currencies are property, not currency, for tax purposes. Below is a breakdown of common crypto transactions and how they are taxed:

Transaction type:	How the transaction is taxed:
Trading cryptocurrency	Capital gains taxes (either short term or long-term depending on holding period)
Receiving payments in crypto in exchange for products or services or as salary	Ordinary income, potentially subject to self-employment taxes
Cryptocurrency received through mining	Ordinary income subject to self-employment taxes
Converting cryptocurrency into USD or another currency	Capital gains taxes
Spending your coins on goods and services (For example, you bought 1 coin for $100, it is now worth $200, and you buy a $200 gift card with it. You made $100 taxable gain)	Capital gains taxes (either short term or long-term depending on holding period)

Furthermore, there are no exemptions for transactions below a certain threshold. Paying somebody for a service, even a coffee, will result in a capital gain or loss.

Purchasing and selling crypto within a year generates a short-term capital gain. This means that the gain will be taxed at an ordinary income rate of 0% to 37%, depending on your tax bracket. When Crypto is held for more than one year before selling it, it will be taxed at the long-term capital gains rate which is between 0% and 20%, plus a 3.8% Net Investment Income Tax depending on your income.

To determine how long you have held a cryptocurrency, you can either use First In First Out (FIFO) accounting, Last In First Out (LIFO) accounting, or specific identification. IRS guidance from 2019 confirmed that you can use specific identification, which can help some traders save on tax although it can be difficult and costly to track. You can use whichever of these three accounting methods you want, as long as you do it consistently. If you go back to amend previous returns and switch the accounting method to save on tax, you will be doing so at a significantly higher audit risk.

Reporting Cryptocurrency Received Via Airdrop

Crypto airdrops can mean a free token or coin for crypto holders. An airdrop may be distributed for a variety of reasons, including marketing purposes, to raise funds, through an exchange, or after a hard fork. However, they are not without tax implications.

The 2019 crypto guidance focused on airdrops as a result of a hard fork. The specifics of tax treatment for other types of airdrops remains unclear. Nonetheless, crypto holders should remember to report any income, gain, or loss from taxable transactions involving virtual currency in their tax return. The IRS confirmed that new cryptocurrency received as a result of a hard fork is ordinary, taxable income. Keep in mind that you must report new cryptocurrency, whether you asked for the airdrop or not. The amount of income that you must report for new cryptocurrency is the cost basis of the crypto at the time that you received it. The cost basis can also be referred to as the fair market value at the time the cryptocurrency was received. According to the IRS, soft forks do not create income because no new cryptocurrency was received.

Crypto Recordkeeping For Taxes

As an owner of cryptocurrency, it is crucial that you keep good records. Programs such as Bitcoin.tax or Cointracking are helpful for this. We recommend keeping detailed records of your cryptocurrency, including:

- Date and time each unit was acquired
- Cost basis of each unit at the time it was acquired
- Date and time each unit was sold, exchanged, or otherwise disposed of
- Fair market value of each unit when sold, exchanged, or otherwise disposed of
- Amount of money or the value of property received for each unit

Your records may also include information such as receipts, evidence of sales, exchanges or other dispositions of your cryptocurrency, and a digital identifier, private key, or public key for each coin.

Chapter 11: Filing Back Taxes And Other Non-Compliance Resolution

Realizing that you owe back taxes and FBARs is enough to make anyone nervous. You may be concerned about having the IRS knocking at your door, being fined thousands of dollars, or even losing your passport. Though these are largely myths, the potential penalties and even legal implications can be alarming.

Penalties And Other Repercussions Of Not Filing

The IRS usually has hefty penalties for failing to file. Delinquent taxpayers face four types of penalties 1) late filing penalties, 2) late payment penalties, 3) interest penalties, and the accuracy related penalty for substantial underpayment penalty.

1. Late filing penalties. The penalty for filing taxes late is 5% of the unpaid tax amount for each month the tax return is late. This is limited to 25% of the unpaid taxes.
2. Late payment penalties. The penalty for failure to pay is 0.5% of the unpaid taxes per month in penalties, with a maximum total of up to 25% of the amount of unpaid taxes.
3. Interest penalties. Interest on owed tax starts accruing on the original due date of the return until the full payment of taxes is made. The interest compounds daily and the rate is determined quarterly based roughly on the interest rate of the market.
4. Accuracy related penalties. The penalty is 20% of the unpaid tax. This is imposed by the IRS for certain taxpayer behavior such as substantial underpayment and negligence.

In short, the penalties for not filing and not paying can be substantial. Furthermore, failing to file a tax return is a federal crime that may result in more fines and even jail time in extreme situations.

US taxpayers who are behind on taxes could come up against other issues. For example, an unpaid tax liability of over $53,000 or more can prevent you from renewing your US passport. In some cases, it could even be revoked. Additionally, Americans who have children that may use college financial aid in the US need proof of being tax compliant to apply.

Lastly, you may also lose out on significant exclusions and deductions, such as the Foreign Earned Income Exclusion (Chapter 3) that could bring your US tax bill to zero. If you have claimed the FEIE in the past and fail to file the next year's return, you may be banned from claiming the exclusion for the next six tax years. The IRS can also disallow the FEIE if you don't file the return within one year of the original due date. Luckily, most delinquent taxpayers qualify for IRS amnesty programs. We explain those below.

Unfortunately, back taxes are not the only issue. US citizens who did not file a Foreign Bank Account Report (FBAR, Chapter 7) could face additional fines. The penalty for not filing FBAR depends on whether the failure to file was willful or non-willful. For willful failure to file an FBAR, the penalty can be up to $129,210 (2021) or 50% of the foreign account balance, whichever is higher. For non-willful failure to file an FBAR, the penalty can be up to $12,921.

Failure to report foreign financial assets on Form 8938 can result in penalties in additional penalties. For this form, penalties start at $10,000 and can reach up to

$50,000.

Options For Catching Up On Back Taxes

Americans who are behind on taxes have a few options for catching up. Which one is right for you will vary depending on the specifics of your situation.

The Streamlined Compliance Program is by far the most common way to catch up on back taxes for filers who are considered low risk. It requires filing 3 years of back taxes, and 6 years of FBAR, and signing a sworn affidavit. The Streamlined Compliance Program is not the only option for getting back into tax compliance, but it is the most common. The majority of delinquent tax filers can use it and avoid penalties.

Next, the OVDP Replacement is an option for delinquent US taxpayers with offshore assets. The original Offshore Voluntary Disclosure Program (OVDP) was closed in 2018. However, the new Voluntary Disclosure Compliance Program is for offshore assets that taxpayers willfully did not report. Unlike with the old OVDP, the IRS examiner can now impose significant tax penalties and even criminal charges. This approach carries significant risks.

Additionally, some taxpayers do a Quiet Disclosure. This is not an official IRS program. A Quiet Disclosure is when either a taxpayer submits only the current tax year without correcting the previous years or when a taxpayer submits their back tax returns without using a compliance program or notifying the IRS. While this sounds simple, it may put you at greater risk of further scrutiny and provides no waiver of penalties.

Generally speaking, Quiet Disclosures are not worth the risk. When possible, an IRS program to get into compliance is much better. If you are ineligible for a compliance program and only a year behind, then your best option may be to go ahead and file that missing return and apply for a first-time penalty abatement waiver, if applicable.

US taxpayers who are caught up on tax returns but are behind on information returns (such as the FBAR and Form 8938), may be able to file a delinquent international information return. If using this program, you should include a reason for why you did not submit the returns. Though, the IRS can assess penalties without regard to the reason for not filing.

If the IRS has already contacted you or if you willfully failed to file, immediately seek the counsel of an experienced tax accountant or tax attorney to evaluate your options.

If you're not sure about your filing obligations, visit Chapter 2 for a recap. For more about the FBAR, check Chapter 7.

IRS Streamlined Compliance Procedure

The Streamlined Compliance Procedure is a way for individuals to catch up on back taxes and FBARs without incurring high penalties. This procedure is only for taxpayers whose failure to file and report was not willful. You cannot use the program if you're currently under examination by the IRS.

Taxpayers who use the Streamlined Compliance Procedure need to file three years of past due tax returns and six prior years of FBARs. In other words, someone using the Streamlined Compliance Procedure at the end of 2020 (after the October 15 filing deadline) would file returns for 2020, 2019, and 2018. If it was before the filing deadline, they would need to file 2021 (which is the current year) and 2020-2018 (the three prior years according to the program). They would file FBARs for 2020, 2019, 2018, 2017, 2016, and 2015. Someone filing before the June 15 deadline would be required to file an extension for the 2020 tax year. They would then file 2020 normally and file their 2017-2019 returns and 2014-2019 FBARs under the program. In addition to filing prior years under the Streamlined Program, taxpayers should file the current year return normally.

If you owe previous Form 8938s to report your foreign assets, they need to be included with your tax returns.

Taxpayers who use the Streamlined Compliance Procedure only need to pay back taxes owed plus interest. The penalties for failure to file and late payment are waived. Likewise, fines for delinquent FBARs are also waived. Importantly, the IRS streamlined procedure does not trigger an audit. Instead, the returns are processed as usual and have the same chance of being selected for an audit as a timely-filed return.

US persons using the streamlined procedure must fill out Form 14653. In this form, they write a narrative about why they failed to report their income and information. It is important to work with a tax expert on this form because it is one of the most important parts of the Streamlined Compliance Procedure.

If you are eligible, it is important to act soon since IRS amnesty programs are only available for a limited amount of time. Once the IRS determines that enough time has passed for taxpayers to gain awareness and use the procedure, then they may change or close the procedure.

Chapter 12: Tax For US Business Owners Abroad

For US business owners who live abroad, the jurisdiction they choose to incorporate in will have lasting tax and legal implications. The primary decision you will need to make is when to incorporate, and whether the United States or a foreign country makes the most sense for you.

In some cases, your decision may be obvious. For example, if you are selling on Amazon Europe, you would want a European company for VAT and payment reasons.

Likewise, one would set up a US LLC to sell in the US. For others, the decision is less clear. If you're a freelancer or someone who can work from anywhere, you will likely have a variety of options.

This chapter will cover some of the most important considerations for incorporating and running a business abroad. But ultimately, the best approach will be customized and vary from individual to individual. This is a situation where there is no one-size-fits-all solution. Don't let this deter you from incorporating. Not incorporating at all is one of the biggest mistakes we see business owners make.

Most Common Mistakes When Incorporating

You can steer clear of many issues through careful planning. Working with a structuring expert will help you to select the right structure and put the best plan in place to avoid these common mistakes when setting up a business abroad.

Below are seven of the mistakes we see most frequently when selecting an offshore jurisdiction:

1. Choosing The Wrong Jurisdiction

You may have seen articles or forum discussions on "the best offshore jurisdiction". But unfortunately, there is no one-size-fits-all answer. Which jurisdiction is the best for you depends on your business and your objectives for going offshore. Places like St. Kitts & Nevis and the Cook Islands offer the most asset protection while credit card processing is easier in Hong Kong and Singapore. Some countries in the Caribbean have an easier set up process and lower annual fees. However, the banking is not as good, so there are trade-offs.

2. Not Setting Up The Right Business Structure

Many entrepreneurs and investors start without a formal legal structure or outgrow their initial structure. Still, almost every investor and entrepreneur can realize tax savings, legal protections, and other benefits by operating with the right business structure. Whether you are seeking outside investment, if your investors/owners are US persons/companies/trusts/funds, and what the ownership structure is, it will all factor into the optimal business structure to use.

3. Overlooking Transfer Pricing

Understanding transfer pricing is important when there is a relationship between a US-based company and a foreign company owned by the same person or company. In this situation, a transfer pricing study must be performed in order to document this relationship and to ensure that an arm's length transaction/price is given, meaning that goods or services are exchanged between the two companies at fair market value based on comparable transactions and competitors. This is an audit red flag as the IRS is aware of people setting up this type of relationship to shift profits from the US to a low tax jurisdiction.

4. Being Unaware Of Reporting Requirements

There are many reporting requirements in regard to disclosing foreign companies (Form 5471), bank accounts (FBAR/Form 8938), and overseas transfers (Form 926) which are important to file correctly. Form 8858 for a disregarded entity or Form 8865 for foreign partnership might be applicable as well in some cases. Make sure you know the IRS classification of your entity and are filing correctly as failure to do so can result in $10,000 fines. In addition, you may have reporting requirements in your offshore jurisdiction.

5. Not Keeping Expense Records For US Tax Reporting

The US IRS has the right to audit any business owned by a US person, foreign and domestic. Therefore, you must report expenses and maintain records, just like you would for a US business. Please keep receipts and maintain good books for your foreign company. If you have wrong information on Form 5471 you are still subject to the $10,000 fine, even if you file on time.

6. Overlooking The Implications Of Foreign Partners

To be a CFC or not to be a CFC, that is the question. If the entity is owned by over 50% US shareholders and under 11 shareholders in total, the foreign company is considered a Controlled Foreign Corporation (CFC). This changes both reporting and tax implications for the company and transactions with related parties. If possible, keep US ownership at 50% or under to make your life easier. Also, watch out for constructive ownership rules about how foreign relatives count towards your ownership percentage.

7. Inadvertently Becoming A PFIC

If you own a foreign company that holds passive investments, whether stocks, bonds or real estate, it can be considered a Passive Foreign Investment Company (PFIC). This will have negative consequences for you when you sell the company. There are several ways to avoid PFIC treatment such as the check the box election on Form 8832.

Having A US LLC Or S Corporation While Living Abroad

Other times, a US company may actually be more optimal than a foreign company for a US expat. US companies offer many advantages, including more flexibility with your retirement planning.

Before we go too much further, here's something to remember: You can still claim the FEIE even if you run a US company. This is something a lot of accountants get wrong. For questions to ask before hiring an accountant, visit Chapter 16.

LLC vs S Corp – Which Is The Best Small Business Structure

Most US entrepreneurs and small business owners set up an LLC when they want to "make it legal". LLCs are easy and comparably cheap to set up and operate. S Corporations have similarities with LLCs, but also some distinct characteristics, that may be more advantageous for a business.

LLCs and S Corps have a lot in common. They both offer limited liability protection, which protects the personal assets of the owner against debts, losses, and any court rulings against the business. They are also both considered separate legal entities, which means that at the state level they are legal entities that are separate from the owner (although US sole owner LLCs are included on an individual's personal tax return). Both types of entities have to comply with state-mandated formalities, such as filing annual reports and paying the fees.

Finally, LLCs and S Corps don't pay income taxes at the business level on the federal level. In some states and cities such as New York City, Missouri, and California, S Corps are taxed. Instead, business profit or loss is passed through to the owners' personal tax returns. Any tax is reported and paid at the individual level. This is known as pass through taxation.

Advantages Of An LLC

LLCs offer some advantages that S Corps do not. One of them is that there is no restriction of ownership. This means that the members of the LLC can be non-US citizens or non-residents. This offers flexibility for individuals who have a non-resident alien business partner or who work with a non-resident alien spouse. This flexibility also extends to ownership by entities. LLCs can be owned by a corporation and certain types of trusts, while S Corporations cannot.

Another feature is that LLCs can have subsidiaries without restriction. This is a useful benefit for individuals who plan to own multiple brands (such as e-commerce) or multiple properties for real estate investing. This allows them to separate each income stream and their associated liability.

Finally, LLCs are a simple structure. They require less paperwork, internal formalities are only recommended, but not required for LLCs. (Although this can be a disadvantage as it often leads to a lack of documentation of agreements and business decisions). They also offer less complicated tax filings. An LLC is either recognized on the Schedule C of an individual return or as a partnership if multiple partners. An S Corp must always file an 1120S which creates an extra filing obligation.

An individual owner of an LLC does not pay unemployment or disability taxes, but that also means that the owner is not entitled to state unemployment or disability benefits. They are also not required to take a minimum salary and deal with payroll taxes.

Advantages Of An S Corporation

One of the notable advantages of an S Corporation is that it can sell stock, which can be traded freely as long as IRS requirements are met. An LLC by comparison can only sell interest in the company. Therefore, an S Corp is more appealing to investors, not only due to its ability to issue stock, but also because S Corps have a more rigid management structure and more extensive reporting requirements. Those required formalities include adopting bylaws, holding initial and annual director and shareholder meetings, and keeping meeting minutes with corporate records. However, an S Corp can only be owned by US citizens and resident aliens and it has restrictions on the type of entity which can hold it. Non-resident aliens cannot own an S Corp.

S Corporations also offer reduced self-employment taxes. An S Corp can pay a reasonable salary to its working owner(s). The salary paid to the owner is a deductible business expense which will limit the amount of self-employment taxes (Social Security and Medicare taxes) that are due, as those only apply to the amount of salary taken. The remaining net income of the S Corp is considered a distribution and not subject to self-employment tax. This is the main advantage why people choose an S Corp as a business structure.

Reasonable salary depends on the net income, location, and industry. You should also reference the US Department of Labor's Bureau of Labor Statistics, employment agencies, recruiting firms and market analysis to see compensation rates for comparable services.

As you can see, you have various points to consider when selecting a business structure. Many entrepreneurs start out with an LLC and switch later to an S Corp.

Why And When To Switch From LLC To S Corp

Many US entrepreneurs set up an LLC in the beginning, because it is straightforward and not too expensive. Generally, this is a good approach for the start, as LLCs offer liability protection and other advantages. However, entrepreneurs are often not aware that with increasing income, switching from LLC to S Corp makes financial sense.

One of the biggest and most well-known advantages of an S corporation over an LLC is saving on self-employment tax. With an LLC, the income passes through to the owner, who has to pay 15.3% self-employment tax on the entire net profit. If the owner resides abroad, the Foreign Earned Income Exclusion can minimize income tax but not self-employment tax. With an S Corp on the other hand, the owner can take a salary from the profits, pay social security and Medicare tax only on the salary, and still apply the Foreign Earned Income Exclusion to minimize income tax. To give an example, if an LLC that is making $100,000 in net income and is paying $14,129 in self-employment taxes is converted to an S Corp, whose owner takes a $60,000 salary (supportable by market research), then only $9,180 in Medicare and Social Security is paid, generating $5,039 in savings.

From a tax perspective, it makes sense to convert an LLC into an S Corp when the tax savings exceed the administration costs and headaches of an S Corp, such as payroll and filing an additional tax return (if only one owner). With an S Corp, a separate Form 1120S needs to be filed for the entity, with each owner getting a K1 statement to be file on their personal return. In general, with around $40,000 net income you should consider converting to S Corp. Depending on your circumstances, the breakeven point could even be as low as $25,000 net income. Of course, the details depend on a variety of factors, including the salary amount and the state of incorporation.

The owner of an S Corp can take a salary from the profits. What is considered a reasonable salary depends on the net income and industry, so it is difficult to give a target dollar figure. You may hear the general rule of thumb that salary can be two thirds of net income. However, take this with a grain of salt. The salary amount is very subjective relative to industry standards and should be supportable. If the owner qualifies for the Foreign Earned Income Exclusion, then he or she can exclude up to $108,700 (2021) of the salary from income tax. This affects the breakeven calculation.

State tax rules also impact the potential savings for switching from LLC to S Corp. Some states tax at the S Corp level and the individual shareholder level, for example California and New York City. If you are incorporated in one of those states, the tax savings for switching from LLC to S Corp diminishes. It is generally still worthwhile to convert to save taxes as well as retirement savings options.

How To Convert An LLC To S Corporation

For federal tax purposes you can simply make an election for the LLC to be taxed as an S Corporation. Usually, all you need to do is fill out a Form 2553 and send it to the IRS. Once you have received confirmation, your entity can immediately classify as an S Corp, effective to the date of the election, not the date you received confirmation.

It is important to note that one must convert to an S Corp by March 15 in order to be applicable for that tax year, or within 75 days of opening the LLC to be applicable for the year of opening. If you miss this deadline, you may apply for late election relief if you have a valid reason for missing the deadline.

Keep in mind though that with this approach you don't change the actual entity type, only the federal tax classification. Even though the IRS classifies the LLC as S Corp, it is still an LLC and may be taxed as such by the state where it is formed. To change the actual entity structure, you have to formally change the LLC to a Corporation with the formation state. Some states offer a formal conversion process, while others require a workaround.

Disadvantages Of C Corporations

Generally, C Corporations are not that common among Americans abroad because they are taxed twice. With a C Corp, you will be taxed at the corporate level and at an individual level.

A C Corporation may be a good option for a larger company with more shareholders that is seeking venture capital investments or investments from non-resident aliens who don't want to file a US tax return. Keep in mind that NRAs may still need to file a US tax return if they take a dividend and qualify to get a tax refund from their automatic withholding. C Corps are ideal for businesses seeking investors because the structure makes it easier for investors to purchase and sell stocks. It's also a popular option for NRAs who are investing in US real estate. NRAs who own C Corps that do not distribute earnings and have no US individuals associated with the entity do not have individual tax return obligations. Moreover, if they pay themselves a salary, it's not taxable in the US if it was not earned in the United States.

In some situations, a business may start as an LLC but then convert to a C Corp before selling or if they are going to seek outside investment. However, C Corps are also more complicated and require more work to maintain. They must have a board of directors and annual meetings that include the board, directors, and shareholders. Minutes also need to be recorded.

Having A Foreign Business

Many websites advertise the tax savings of going offshore. An offshore business structure is not just for the Apples and Googles of the world. Even small business owners and solo entrepreneurs can benefit.

Let's look at an example of an entrepreneur with an online business to illustrate the potential tax savings with an offshore structure. A US citizen living abroad, let's call him Mark, owns a web development business, which he operates as a Wyoming LLC. He makes $190,000 in earnings and has $40,000 expenses, so a net profit of $150,000. Since an LLC is a pass-through entity (and he didn't elect to be taxed as an S Corporation), the profit passes through to Mark's personal income. He meets the requirements for claiming the Foreign Earned Income Exclusion, so he doesn't have to pay income tax on the first about $120,000 [$108,700 of Foreign Earned Income

Exclusion plus $12,550 of the standard deduction for Single filers (2021 tax year limits)].

Because he is in the 24% tax bracket, he pays about $7,200 income tax for the non-excluded $30,000 income. In addition, since he is considered self-employed, he also has to pay 15.3% self-employment tax (Social Security and Medicare) on his entire earned income of $150,000, so about $21,092. So, in total, he pays approximately $28,000 tax to the US.

While the LLC structure provides Mark with liability protection, it does not optimize his tax situation. He could optimize the self-employment tax if his LLC elects to be taxed as an S Corporation. Mark could then pay himself a (reasonable) salary below the FEIE limit, let's say $70,000, which would be subject to Social Security and Medicare tax, about $10,000.

The remaining $80,000 earnings are considered a profit distribution and hence not subject to paying 15.3% tax for Medicare and Social Security. It is however subject to income tax on the amount above the $120,000 (FEIE plus standard deduction) due to the fact he is the sole shareholder and primary employee of the company. At the 24% tax bracket, this is $7,200, as in the previous example, bringing his total tax burden to about $17,200. This simple election to be taxed as a corporation could save him roughly $11,000 per year.

Mark could optimize his tax burden even further with the right offshore business structure. If he had an offshore structure in a low or no-tax jurisdiction that is owned by his US C Corporation, he could benefit from the new GILTI tax rate of only 10.5% if his business meets certain requirements.

He would also not pay any Social Security or Medicare taxes as he is being paid from a foreign company. He can take a $108,700 salary which is not taxable under the Foreign Earned Income Exclusion, given that he qualifies. The remaining $40,000 profit of the company would be subject to the 10.5% effective tax rate of the corporation under GILTI, $4,200.

He can receive this money in the form of dividends. Those would be taxed at a rate of 0%, 15%, or 20%, depending on his tax rate. Assuming he takes out the entire $40,000 profit as dividend and is in the 15% tax bracket, Mark pays another $6,000 in tax. His tax total would be just over $10,000, compared to almost $30,000 without a good structure in place. Mark would benefit from significant tax savings, even when you take into account the cost of setting up and maintaining the offshore business.

The right foreign structure not only gives huge tax savings but also asset protection. Of course, every situation is unique. Depending on your income, type of business, your needs, and other factors, your outcome could be quite different. A structuring expert can help you evaluate different onshore and offshore scenarios and advice on a full plan that includes tax optimization, asset protection, retirement planning, and more.

Reporting Requirements

Owners of foreign business will likely encounter more than a few reporting obligations. They usually need to disclose their foreign company on Form 5471, report qualifying bank accounts and other financial assets (FBAR and Form 8938) and report overseas transfers and contributions (Form 926). This is most common in the first year when capitalizing a foreign corporation. Depending on the entity, other forms such as Form 8858 for disregarded entities or Form 8865 for foreign partnership might be needed too. It's important to make sure you know the IRS classification of your entity and file correctly. Failure to do so can result in $10,000 fines. This penalty is applied per missing form. When people have multiple foreign corporations and failed to file, we've seen up to $140,000 in fines from the IRS. (Thankfully, we have been able to get the fines abated previously).

In addition, there may be reporting requirements in your offshore jurisdiction.

Global Intangible Low-Taxed Income (GILTI)

In 2017, the Tax Cuts and Jobs Act made significant changes to the taxation of businesses. It ended tax deferral for foreign companies and also introduced a new tax on any new foreign income that international companies earn, called GILTI (Global Intangible Low-Taxed Income). GILTI represents a new category of income. It is income earned by foreign affiliates of US companies from intangible assets (for example, a trademark or copyright). Generally, GILTI is reported as a flow through to the owner's tax return.

Under the GILTI rules though, certain US shareholders of C Corporations can deduct 50% of their GILTI, which halves the effective corporate tax rate to 10.5%. Furthermore, they can claim foreign tax credits, lowering the US federal income tax due even further. This is a significant reduction over the previous 35% corporate tax rate and still substantially lower than the new 21% corporate tax rate.

Since the Tax Cuts and Jobs Act, you cannot defer taxes on foreign earnings anymore. However, you gain the flexibility to move the money as you see fit. You can now decide if you want to keep your taxed earnings overseas or bring it to the US, with no additional tax impact as a dividend from a foreign subsidiary to a US C Corp, is taxed at 0%. (Although declaring a dividend to the US shareholder will be taxed at income tax rates of 0% to 37% depending on the tax bracket and whether or not the foreign corporation is located in a treaty country).

Of course, there are requirements to qualify for the low 10.5% tax rate. Just as for the previous tax deferral, the lower GILTI tax rate only applies to international businesses that do not engage in US trade or business. If you have operations, an office or warehouse in the US, or a "dependent agent" that works for you exclusively, you have a US presence and cannot take advantage of the 10.5% GILTI tax rate.

When the remaining earnings after the corporate tax are distributed to shareholders as dividends, shareholders will pay tax on those dividends. The qualified dividend tax rates remained unchanged at 0%, 15%, and 20%, depending on their personal income tax bracket.

Higher GILTI Tax For LLCs And S Corps

The GILTI rules apply a higher tax rate to GILTI attributed to individuals and trusts who own controlled foreign corporation (CFC) stock (either directly or through LLCs or S Corps) than to C Corporation shareholders.

Previously, a US person generally only had to pay tax on income earned through a foreign corporation when he received that income as a dividend. Now under the new rules, if a US person (not a C Corp) is a 10% shareholder of a Controlled Foreign Corporation (CFC), he or she must include their portion of the foreign income on their personal tax return, regardless of whether or not it was received as a distribution to shareholders. This income could be taxed up to a whopping 37% if they are in the highest tax bracket.

Owning shares in a CFC either directly or through an LLC or S Corp may expose you to a higher tax rate than owning the same shares through a C Corp. As a non-C Corporation US shareholder of a foreign company, you can take steps to reduce your tax rate by electing Section 962 treatment or by owning the Controlled Foreign Corporation (CFC) through a US C Corporation.

Section 962 election allows the individual to be taxed as a corporation. This would lower your tax rate to 21%. If you are paying taxes in a foreign country above 18.9% then you could receive the high tax exception or use the foreign tax credit, which means you would not pay any US corporate tax on the earnings. However, if you do not pay taxes locally, you generally would not want to make this election and putting a C Corp in place that owns the foreign company allows you to take advantage of the lower corporate tax rates.

Furthermore, in a non-tax treaty country, you will also pay ordinary income rates for the dividends taken rather than 15% or 20% qualified dividend tax rate.

Even if you don't take advantage of the lower C Corp tax rates, there is a silver lining. While you may pay more as an individual owner than as a C Corp with GILTI, you won't need to worry about dividend taxation.

Choosing A Foreign Jurisdiction

Choosing the right jurisdiction is not magic or luck. Don't just follow the most popular or well-known option or rely on the latest online advice. Instead, the right jurisdiction depends on your specific goals for offshoring.

Here are 10 offshoring criteria to help prioritize your objectives:

1. Reputation

Will the offshore business be your international "face" to customers and business partners? Then a highly reputable jurisdiction like Hong Kong may be a good choice, even so, reporting and audit requirements are more onerous there, compared to other jurisdictions. Luxembourg, Malta, and Singapore are also a few jurisdictions with very good reputations but are extremely expensive to open and operate in, costing over $10,000 annually in certain cases. Places such as Panama or Cyprus may look good on paper but have a history of money laundering and can be frowned upon by some foreign governments and banks.

Keep in mind that a business in a jurisdiction that does not meet global financial requirements may receive more scrutiny from tax and financial authorities. Therefore, it is wise to generally stay away from those "black-listed" offshore jurisdictions and you should check if there is a blacklist of countries or "fiscal paradises" released by the country that you claim residency. For example, for a property investor in Portugal, we may set up the holding company in Dominican Republic because many of the traditional holding company jurisdictions were blacklisted.

2. Tax Optimization

Is there a way to be domiciled in a lower tax jurisdiction or even no tax jurisdiction? The answer to this question depends on where the operations of your company are located and the type of business you have.

Tax havens such as the Caymans or the British Virgin Islands (BVI) offer no income tax for foreign businesses among other advantages. However, its incorporation fees are not the lowest, with a cost of $1,500-2,000 for quality services. Furthermore, for certain business activities such as banking, trust management, or investment advisory services, a BVI company requires a license.

In addition, not only the jurisdiction where the company is incorporated but also the country where the business operates or where the active shareholders reside can levy taxes. There may be local CFC laws on top of the US structuring considerations. Because of this, choosing the right jurisdiction and ownership percentage (when possible) can drastically alter the taxes due.

3. Available Tax Treaties

Where do you operate your business? Are you importing/exporting, or do you operate or sell in various jurisdictions via independent or dependent agents?

Having a tax treaty with the jurisdiction in which your corporation is set up can help avoid being taxed in both jurisdictions. Selecting an offshore jurisdiction with a double tax treaty may be particularly beneficial for financial holding and investment activities, holding IP, leasing, and franchising (royalty collection), as well as establishing a tax home/permanent establishment in that jurisdiction.

Many countries withhold taxes on certain types of income derived in their jurisdiction, for example for royalties or dividend/interest income. A tax treaty usually reduces the tax withholding. Most tax treaties, but not all, provide tax relief for the beneficial owner of the income. For example, US shareholders receive qualified dividend treatment for dividend payments for companies in a tax treaty jurisdiction. This can significantly reduce the taxes from ordinary income rates to between 0% to 37% depending on the tax bracket.

4. Banking

Do you want to run income and expenses through an offshore bank? Do you need PayPal or a credit card processor such as Stripe? Are you running a business in need of a specialized credit card processor due to high-risk clients or products? Understanding your specific banking requirements will determine the best banking jurisdiction. This may or may not be the same offshore location as for your company.

You don't have to bank in the same country that your offshore company is incorporated. However, not every bank will want to deal with a company incorporated in some offshore jurisdictions. FATCA and CRS, KYC (Know Your Customer) compliance is becoming stricter, which means banks are more selective about who they have relationships with and take on as clients. The opening minimum deposit, your willingness to travel and the source of your income or funds are some of the factors that banks look at during this process. In some cases, we structure the credit card processing through a US LLC disregarded entity or through a sister company C Corp in order to provide the client with the best solution for their business.

Banking options are becoming more limited as regulations increase and offshore jurisdictions receive more scrutiny.

5. Asset Protection

Do you want to keep your assets out of reach from civil creditors and litigation? Some jurisdictions, such as Nevis and the Cook Islands offer greater protection against civil creditors than, let's say, the US. Iron-clad asset protection will not necessarily shield assets from taxation though.

Asset protection usually involves a Foreign Grantor Trust to hold the assets. The trust is the owner of an offshore LLC (usually in a different jurisdiction), which is the holder of the assets. An offshore trust cannot be used like an offshore bank account, where you can withdraw money at any time. You as the trustor are renouncing control of the assets into the trust. You no longer own these assets. The trust owns these assets, and they are overseen by the Trustee. The deed of trust entered into with your foreign Trustee governs how funds are distributed and decisions are dictated by the "statement of wishes" document. Without the deed of trust, you would be missing a crucial layer of protection.

Setting up and maintaining an asset protection trust does not come cheap. It involves considerable planning and specialized expertise.

6. Accounting And Reporting Requirements

Do you want to keep the paperwork and reporting to a minimum? Hong Kong would not be your first choice then, since they require annual audits. Many of the Caribbean locations, on the other hand, only require a registered agent to collect your mail. If you are in search of investors, then an investor-friendly jurisdiction like BVI or Cayman has the laws and more robust legal and professional services to help in compliance.

As a US citizen, keep in mind that any type of offshore structure will increase your reporting requirements in the US. You may have to file a myriad of forms with the IRS and Treasury, included but not limited to Forms 5471, 926, 8858, 8865, 3520, 3520A, FBAR, etc. Ideally, your advisor for business structuring is well versed in US tax implications (like us).

7. Privacy

Is your most important goal to shield assets and information from the prying eyes of others? Staying anonymous is not possible. Global anti-money laundering laws (AML) and other regulations to prevent identity theft, criminal activities, and terrorism require that your identity is shared with the agent (for incorporation) and financial institutions. It is no longer a game of "hide and seek" but now it is "show and tell."

Some jurisdictions don't require your information to be shared with the local government, or even prohibit the agent from publicly disclosing your documents, except for certain inquiries including tax inquiries. This can however change at any time.

Bottom line is that while you can shield your business or assets from public disclosure, you will need to disclose the ultimate beneficial owners to the IRS, other foreign governments, and banks which your structure has a connection with.

8. Ease Of Set Up

Are you looking to form an offshore business quickly with minimal capital requirements? Jurisdictions like the US or Nevis allow you to form a business with minimal capital and paperwork. Most of the time, you can even set up remotely.

Singapore and Luxembourg, on the other hand, require a resident to be the signatory of all paperwork, meaning increased cost and bureaucracy.

Even the cheapest and easiest offshore company formation can end up costing you a lot of money if not done correctly. For US citizens, any offshoring increases US reporting requirement and failure to comply can result in stiff penalties.

9. Operating Cost

Are business formation and ongoing maintenance costs a major concern? If this is a concern of yours, you may want to stay clear of locations such as Hong Kong and Malta that require tax reporting, annual audits, etc., which can quickly add up. However, these reporting requirements give more credence to doing business in these jurisdictions if you have clients that believe this is important.

Belize, Nevis, Saint Lucia are jurisdictions with low fees, where you can incorporate for around $1,500 and have ongoing registration and maintenance for about the same. The opening process is simple, and the renewal is even simpler, just pay your bill and keep the company registered. If you are just holding assets and not doing a lot of transactions, these jurisdictions are perfect.

10. Business Operations

Does your business require local employees and/or business interactions with specific time zones? Selecting an offshore location within a similar time zone and language helps with every-day business interactions. Availability of local talent eliminates the need for costly expat hires, such as in BVI and Cayman where there are many service providers. However, if you need native English speakers or don't want to call Asia at midnight if you live in the US, you may have to consider different jurisdictions.

Some jurisdictions such as Singapore and Luxembourg even require a registered agent representative, meaning not only do you need an address but also someone to represent you and be on the hook if there are any financial misgivings. This can add a large additional cost if you don't have any local contacts to represent you.

Lastly, when selecting a jurisdiction, don't overlook the political and economic stability of the country. This is a must-have criterion. No matter what your goals for offshoring are, you don't want to find yourself in an economic crash or unfavorable political change that can hurt your business or assets.

As you can see, the secret to choosing the right offshore jurisdiction is being clear on your objectives for offshoring. We recommend evaluating each criteria and rank-ordering them by priority. This priority list will then drive a shortlist of suitable offshore jurisdictions. At times, you may find that a combination of offshore structures yields the best results for your business, for example incorporating in one country and banking in another. This adds of course more complexity and requires additional considerations to ensure that the jurisdictions are compatible.

An experienced business structurer can help you weigh the pros and cons of each option, understand the potential tax impact, etc. If you need help going through this process, please let us know. We have set up offshore structures in many different jurisdictions and have a global network of partners to support any required local activities.

FBAR For Business Owners

Though many people think of the FBAR as only applicable to individuals, it also applies to US entities. A US entity is any corporation, partnership, LLC, trust, or estate formed under US law.

The requirements for filing are the same for individuals and entities. On the Foreign Bank Account Report (FBAR), US persons must report foreign financial accounts that they have a financial interest in or signature authority over if the combined accounts exceed the threshold.

To calculate the value of the accounts, take the highest balance of each account during the year, and combine them. If the aggregate highest balances of the accounts are over $10,000, then you have exceeded the threshold and need to file an FBAR.

Whether you will need to submit an FBAR for your US entity depends on the amount of voting power you have, the number of shares, and several other factors. How your ownership is measured depends on the type of entity.

The penalty for non-willful failure to file an FBAR is $12,921. For willful failure to file, the penalty is $129,210 or 50% of the account balance, whichever is higher. Offenders may face criminal prosecution and jail time. Remember, offshore financial accounts and assets are not tax-exempt. Attempting to hide or failing to report offshore financial accounts may result in penalties.

You may also have to report your foreign assets. The Foreign Account Tax Compliance Act (FATCA) requires that certain US taxpayers and businesses report foreign assets that exceed the threshold on Form 8938. Stocks, bonds, mutual funds, life insurance or annuities, interest in foreign entities, and more are all reportable on this form.

Offshore Banking

Offshore banking is any banking outside of an individuals' home country. Most offshore banking is done at regular banks in foreign countries. You can use offshore bank accounts for personal, business, or investment purposes. Private banking may also an option. It is not true that only the incredibly wealthy or criminals use offshore bank accounts. Opening an offshore account can be an important investment and diversification strategy and a good business move for many.

Offshore banking can offer benefits such as higher interest rates, easier access to investments abroad, and a reduced tax burden when combined with proper planning. It also offers long-term advantages for estate planning, diversification, and a hedge against risk for estate planning.

Contrary to common belief, offshore banking is legal and there are many legitimate reasons to bank in a foreign country. We have clients who have wanted to diversify outside the US both in terms of asset protection and currency risk. Some have used offshore structures and bank accounts to invest in alternative investments such as cryptocurrency while others like the diversification of having accounts not regulated by the US government (although they still report them). We have also had clients open foreign bank accounts in countries such as Georgia, New Zealand, Peru, and Brazil in order to capitalize on high interest rates. There are many advantages to owning a foreign bank account and our clients have benefitted from this.

Benefits of Banking Offshore

The benefits of an offshore bank account vary based on the individual and their goals. In terms of growth, offshore bank accounts may offer higher interest rates for deposits and investments, easier access to international investments, and optimized taxation when combined with the correct structure. From a protection perspective, offshore banking has many potential advantages including:

- Increased privacy and confidentiality
- Tax-efficient estate planning
- Protection against capital controls or government seizure
- Asset protection in case of lawsuit or divorce
- Diversification of funds into safer bank systems in case of instability in your home country
- Currency diversification in case of inflation, currency collapse, or economic disaster

Disadvantages Of Offshore Bank Accounts

Offshore bank accounts also have disadvantages. They may have higher minimum deposits, be costly to visit, incur bank fees to open and maintain the account, and could require significant documentation. In some countries, including the United States, ownership or control of a foreign financial account may trigger reporting obligations. US persons may need to report their foreign financial accounts and assets on the Foreign Bank Account Report (FBAR) and Form 8938. Because of these factors, it is important that individuals and business owners are strategic about which offshore bank accounts they open and why.

Which Country Is The Best For Offshore Banking?

Because the banking landscape changes quickly, it's difficult to make generalizations about what countries to bank in or what banks to use. A location that is ideal for banking today, may not be recommended in a few months. The following questions also play a role:

- How much are you willing to deposit? Higher amounts mean more options (and often better service).
- Will you travel to open the account? Most banks require it now due to KYC policies.
- Do you need multi-currency accounts?
- What level of service do you need?
- Do you speak the local language, or will you need banking services in English?
- How much are you willing to pay in banking fees?
- All of the above will affect where and which bank you should use.

The best jurisdiction for offshore banking depends on the individual. When evaluating where to open an account overseas, you should consider personal and professional goals as well as the jurisdiction's suitability. The reputation of the jurisdiction, available tax treaties, economic and political stability, asset protection laws, privacy offered, and more are crucial factors. On a personal level, consider your place of citizenship and residence, preferred currencies, and tax residency. Most importantly, evaluate your goals. The needs of a business owner can differ from the needs of an investor.

The amount of time you have available to open the account, whether you are willing to travel, and the amount you can deposit will also play a role. Some foreign banks can process and open accounts within a matter of days. Other banks will take longer to approve and open an account. Because of Know Your Client (KYC) regulations, most banks will require you to appear in person at their office before opening the account.

Keep in mind that the jurisdiction for banking doesn't have to be the same as the company's jurisdiction, though they do influence each other. Some clients prefer diversification where their bank is located in a different country than they are incorporated in. This can sometimes be helpful, or it can make things more difficult. For example, in Singapore, it is very easy to open up a Singapore bank account for a Singapore company. Although this may make you as a reader excited, this also means the government gets to collect taxes as the bank account is considered onshore and the income is taxable. However, Singapore banks will open accounts in Singapore for companies from countries such as Hong Kong, BVI, Cayman. Other jurisdictions they are stricter such as Panama and Belize. Having the right combination of corporate and banking jurisdictions is crucial to any set up.

Amazon Sellers And Other E-Commerce Entrepreneurs

Selling online through Amazon, eBay or any e-commerce site offers great opportunities to make a location-independent income. If you are selling online in the US market and generate a steady income, be aware of the US tax implications.

One of the main concerns for Amazon sellers is the state sales tax. For online sellers who ship solely from one state, the sales tax remains the same. For let's say California, state sales tax is 7.25% plus any local tax if they live in a city that imposes it. For FBA sellers, however, Amazon takes care of shipping the products from their warehouses all over the US. This means that they may be subject to state sales tax in the states where their products are shipped from.

As you can see, sales tax can become very complex. We generally recommend using a service called TaxJar to track and pay sales tax.

In the South Dakota vs. Wayfair case, the US Supreme Court approved the right of states to tax purchases made within the state on products from out-of-state sellers. They can do this even if the company does not have physical presence in the state. Many states now apply state taxes to vendors who exceed a certain dollar sale amount (generally over $100,000) or sell over a certain number of units (typically 200 units).

The right business structure also has a big impact on Amazon seller tax. For non-US sellers, doing business through a US LLC may be the most tax-efficient way. For US persons, there is a choice of a sole member LLC, S Corp, or foreign company. For a single-member LLC, all the income passes through to the owner who then has to declare the income in his or her country of residence. Contrary to common advice, selling through a Belize company that owns the US LLC may not be the income tax-free solution that is often portrayed. In addition, you need to understand the implications of being considered as engaged in US trade or business. A foreign company that owns a US LLC and continuously transacts substantial business in the US, collecting sales tax, and holding inventory in the US to be shipped to US-based customers may be considered engaged in a trade or business in the US. Therefore, the income is considered effectively connected and that the income of the foreign company may be subject to US tax. This applies to Belize and other countries that don't have an income tax treaty with the US, such as Hong Kong, Singapore, or Dubai. If you are in a country that has a tax treaty, income may be exempt. You can avoid US tax if you have an office with a permanent establishment outside of the US as per the tax treaty. We have also seen structures where there is an operating or distribution company outside of the US that sells to the US "retail branch", a company subject to US taxes. These transactions, the relationship and pricing are all dictated by a transfer pricing study.

The Tax Cut and Jobs Act signed in December 2017 brought changes to inventory accounting. If you are a small retailer with less than $25 million in sales and hold inventory, you can elect to treat the inventory as "non-incidental" material and supplies, allowing you to expense the inventory in the year that it was purchased. (Previously the threshold was $1 million). This can simplify your accounting and even result in significant tax savings for retailers and Amazon resellers if they qualify.

Finally, when selling online as a business you can deduct some business expenses. Tax-deductible expenses include:

- Amazon fees
- Cost of Goods Sold (which is not the same as your inventory purchases for the year)
- Shipping expenses
- Home office and office expenses
- Travel to suppliers
- Marketing/branding, e.g., to develop your brand logo when selling your own brand
- Sponsored ads

Chapter 13: Self-Employed Abroad

Oftentimes, individuals begin offering services or freelance before starting a company because incorporating a company involves upfront costs, plus recurring annual fees and filings.

Still, being self-employed can be costly as well. Self-employed individuals often pay more in taxes than their employed or incorporated peers because they typically pay tax on net profit and self-employment taxes.

Taxes For Self-Employed Individuals Abroad

One of the biggest tax burdens self-employed individuals face is self-employment tax (SE tax). When self-employed, you must pay SE tax on your entire net profit, even the amount you can exclude from income tax. The SE tax is a Social Security and Medicare tax for individuals who work for themselves. If you work for a company in the US as an employee, the Social Security and Medicare tax is automatically taken out of your monthly paycheck. As a freelancer or self-employed individual, you are responsible for calculating and paying it quarterly.

The IRS considers you self-employed if you work for yourself, regardless of whether it is full-time or part-time. It also doesn't matter if you are registered as a sole proprietor or not. Even if you have a US LLC you will have to pay SE tax because the LLC income passes through to you as the owner. The only way to optimize for SE tax is to elect your LLC to be taxed as an S Corporation. As a reminder, only a portion of self-employment tax can be reduced. You cannot totally eliminate it. We've seen countless returns incorrectly prepared this way because people mistakenly think they can stop paying self-employment taxes by using an S Corp. This is a common error. Electing for your LLC to be taxed as an S Corp is explained more in Chapter 12 and Chapter 13.

Self-Employment Tax Rate

Though self-employed individuals can claim the Foreign Earned Income Exclusion to reduce their income taxes, it does not reduce self-employment taxes. You must pay self-employment tax on all of your net profit, including the amount excluded under the FEIE.

The self-employment tax rate is 15.3% for the first $142,800 of net income (2021). A 0.9% additional Medicare tax may also apply if your net earnings from self-employment exceed $200,000 if you're a single filer or $250,000 if you're filing jointly.

Let's say you are self-employed abroad and qualify for the Foreign Earned Income Exclusion. Your foreign earned income is $80,000 and your business deductions total $20,000, so your net profit is $60,000. You don't have to pay federal income tax because you can exclude all of your foreign income. But you have to pay the 15.3% self-employment tax on all $60,000 of your net profit.

Self-employed individuals should also be aware that the filing threshold is lower than for employed individuals. The IRS requires that self-employed file a tax return if their annual net earnings are more than $400. Sometimes you have to file even if your earnings are below that if you meet certain requirements.

Reporting Self-Employment Income Earned Abroad

As a self-employed expat, you also need to consider how you will report your income. Unlike a remote employee for a US company, who receives a W-2, a self-employed contractor should receive a Form 1099 NEC. In 2020, the IRS introduced the Form 1099 NEC which is for independent contractors. Form 1099 MISC is for reporting other types of payments such as rent and royalties. 1099 NEC forms only list your gross earnings. Unlike with W-2s, there are no taxes withheld on your behalf. If you earn more than $600 as an independent contractor for a US company, then the company must issue a 1099 form. (Just like with a W-2, a copy of the 1099 Form will be sent to the IRS.) But even if the company fails to give you a 1099, or you earn less than $600 per year with a single company, you still have to disclose the income on your tax return.

PayPal and other electronic payment processors will also send out a Form 1099-K if you meet certain thresholds. According to PayPal, they issue a Form 1099-K to sellers who exceed the IRS thresholds, i.e., when they receive over $20,000 in gross payment volume for the sale of goods or services AND receive over 200 separate payments in the same calendar year. If you don't receive a Form 1099 from them, you need to use your own records to report the income. Many affiliate sites also issue 1099 forms. You can expect that every place that asks for your SSN or tax information, when signing up, could send you – and the IRS – a tax form.

When you receive a 1099 Form from a company you worked for and were paid electronically, for example via PayPal, there is a risk that the same payment is also included in a 1099-K from PayPal. You should compare all 1099 and 1099-K forms carefully against your own records. Be aware that in some cases, for example with Airbnb, the amount on the Form 1099 may include commissions paid to the company that issued the form, instead of just your earnings net of that commission.

Keep also in mind that 1099s sometimes contain errors. Always check them against your own records and request a corrected form if you find a mistake.

Even without a Form 1099, you need to report your foreign self-employment income on your US tax return. You cannot rely on 1099 Forms alone to report your self-employment income for tax. Instead, you have to keep track yourself of your self-employment income and all related expenses.

If you teach English online for a Chinese company while traveling outside the US, do web design or copywriting for international clients, are an independent fashion designer, etc., you will likely not receive any official tax document. That doesn't mean that the income is not subject to the US self-employment tax.

To report income that you didn't receive a Form 1099 or W-2 for, you can use any official or semi-official document or your own spreadsheet. You want to keep track not only of the income you made but also of your expenses and any tax you may have paid on that income. You do not need to submit this to the IRS, but you do need to retain this information in case of audit. If your payments come through PayPal, you can go into the history section and download the history from January 1 to December 31 of the tax year. You can do the same for bank accounts and other financial providers you use for receiving payments. This is much easier if you have separate accounts for your business. We never recommend mixing business and personal finances. For more information on what records US expats need to keep, visit Chapter 17.

Quarterly Estimated Payments

Since self-employed individuals don't have tax deducted from their monthly paycheck, they have to make estimated quarterly payments. Here's how to calculate quarterly estimates for self-employment taxes. Please note this does not include any estimated payments for income taxes. If you make under $108,700 in revenue in 2021 and you qualify for the FEIE for the full year, then you generally would not pay any income tax on the self-employment income. However, every situation is different, so income taxes may be owed depending on your other income sources and amount of time in the US among other factors.

1. Calculate Your Net Earnings

Add up all (expected) income for the year and then subtract all business expenses to calculate your estimated net earnings. Accounting software or at least a simple spreadsheet helps with keeping track of all income and expenses.

2. Estimate Your Taxes And Pay Quarterly Estimated Taxes

Take your estimated net earnings for the year, multiply it by 0.153 for the total self-employment tax, and then divide by 4 to get the quarterly payments. You may also need to estimate for income taxes if you are earning over the foreign earned income exclusion. Quarterly payments are due on April 15, June 15, September 15, and January 15.

If during the year you realize that you will likely make more than estimated, you need to adjust your quarterly payments. Of course, you should also adjust if you think you will make less than expected. Once the year is over and you know your actual income and expenses, you can file your annual tax return and receive a refund if you overpaid.

How To Optimize Self-Employment Tax On Foreign Income

Simply hoping that the US might not know about your foreign self-employment income and therefore not reporting it is asking for trouble.

If you are caught not reporting or under-reporting your income to the IRS, it could be deemed fraudulent and you could be fined heavily. When the IRS suspects fraud, they can go back as many years as they want, even past the three-year statute of limitations. It's important to make sure you report all income properly and accurately.

The only way to optimize self-employment tax is to form a business and elect to be taxed as an S Corporation. Depending on your income level, the cost of forming and maintaining a legal business structure may be more than offset by the savings in self-employment tax.

Also, be aware of any Social Security Totalization Agreements between the US and your residence country. In countries where they exist, you may end up paying to either your host country's government or to the US. This depends on a number of factors unique to each totalization agreement.

If you are in a country where you have to pay social security type taxes locally, you should get a "certificate of coverage" fully translated into English. This ensures the IRS does not ask for SE tax payment as well. Without a Totalization Agreement, you may have to pay into both countries' systems, but you can take the Foreign Tax Credit on paid social security taxes. Chapter 5 has further information about claiming the Foreign Tax Credit.

Chapter 14: Tax Considerations For Digital Nomads

Some members of our team at Online Taxman are nomads, so we've experienced first-hand the unique lifestyle and the issues they face. Digital Nomads are different from the typical expat as they often don't have a fixed foreign home base. Fortunately, nomads can still benefit from expat tax breaks like the Foreign Earned Income Exclusion. But they need to be aware of some of the issues that can arise from perpetual travel.

Structuring their location-independent business in a tax-optimized way is also a primary concern for many nomads.

Tax Home For Claiming The Foreign Earned Income Exclusion

While the Physical Presence Test and the Bona Fide Residence test are often the most talked-about requirements for the Foreign Earned Income Exclusion (FEIE), you also need to have a tax home to qualify.

Unfortunately, defining what constitutes a tax home can be complicated. Essentially, your tax home is your regular place of business or where you regularly live. If you do not have a primary place of business or a place where you regularly live, then your tax home is wherever you work. (As a reminder, your tax home can't be in a foreign country if you live in the United States).

For digital nomads, who live in many places, their tax home is wherever they are. This works well for perpetual travelers. If you spend four months in Thailand and eight months in Colombia, those are your tax homes during the year. Whether you will owe taxes in those countries though depends on their tax laws. (In many countries, income you earn while working from there is taxable there. Often, if you spend more than 183 days in a 365-day period in a country, you become a tax resident there. You need to check the regulations in each country to see if you owe taxes in that country.)

Typically, digital nomads would use the Physical Presence Test to qualify for the FEIE. To qualify via the Bona Fide Residence Test, you need to have a true home base in a foreign country and be able to prove your ties in that country (see Chapter 3 for details). For most digital nomads, that is not an option.

One drawback for location-independent entrepreneurs is that without a regular or main place where they regularly work and live, they are considered transient or itinerant. Therefore, they cannot claim travel expense deductions, because they don't have a home to travel away from. To determine whether you have a primary place or business or work, consider how much time you normal spend in each place, the level of business activity in each location, and whether your income from any of these locations is significant or not.

Still, even if you don't have a fixed place of business you may still have a tax home. To determine if you have a tax home, consider the following:

1. You perform part of your business in your home and use that place for lodging while in the area.
2. You have additional living expenses because you maintain a home in one location and pay for additional living expenses when in a new location for work.
3. You maintain connections to a location that you historically lived in. For example, maybe a member of your family lives at your main home, or you frequently use that home as a place to stay.

If you meet all three of these factors, then you have a tax home. If you meet two of these factors, then you might have a tax home. If you only meet one of these standards, then you are an itinerant and your tax home is wherever you work and you cannot deduct travel expenses that are not specifically related to work.

State Tax

State tax is an area that can be tricky for digital nomads. If you are only temporarily a nomad for a few years and then you return to live in the US, your state may require tax returns for the time you were abroad. The state can argue that it was clear you planned to come back and that you were a resident during your entire time abroad. This is most likely an issue in high tax, "sticky states" such as Virginia and when you maintained ties to the state. If you haven't yet, be sure to read Chapter 8 for a review of state taxation.

For perpetual travelers who previously resided in California, the situation can be especially complex. Current or returning residents of California actually are not allowed to claim the Foreign Earned Income Exclusion or the Foreign Tax Credit, unless they qualify for the California safe harbor rule. To qualify, you need to be outside of California under a contract related to your employment for at least 546 days in a row. If you don't stay out of California for 546 days and come back after anything less, then you will be considered a resident for the entire time. You will be disqualified from this if you have interest, capital gains, divided, royalists, or copyright income of more than $200,000 during any of the years you are abroad. You are also ineligible for the safe harbor rule if the reason you went abroad is to avoid California taxes. Any visits to the state during the safe harbor timeframe should be for 45 days or less.

If you are concerned about state taxes while abroad, review Chapter 8 which covers strategies for moving your tax domicile before moving abroad.

Remote Workers, Freelancers, And Entrepreneurs

As a digital nomad, you may source your income in a variety of ways. You could work remotely for a company, as a freelancer, or be an entrepreneur. Each of these has different tax implications.

Remote Workers

A remote worker may be someone who is employed by a US company or by a foreign company. If you work for a US company, you should receive a W-2 from your employer. If you receive a Form 1099 then you are an independent contractor and you need to pay your own social security and Medicare taxes (see the next section about freelancers for more info). As a W-2 employee, your employer pays half of the social security and Medicare taxes and you pay the remaining half. This is usually withheld automatically from your paycheck.

As an employee of a foreign company, you may or may not receive a statement of your earnings and any foreign taxes paid during the year. If you do not receive a formal statement, you can track how much you earned in an excel spreadsheet or use your pay slips.

Remember, you may also owe taxes in the country of your employer. Be sure to also check if they withheld taxes from your salary during the year. Depending on the tax, you may be able to claim a Foreign Tax Credit for withheld taxes that were not refunded. (See Chapter 5 for more info).

Freelancers/Independent Contractors

As mentioned above, as a freelancer or independent contractor, you receive a Form 1099 from the companies you work for. This means that you are responsible for paying your own self-employment taxes (social security and Medicare). Because your self-employment taxes were not automatically withheld, you may need to make estimated self-employment taxes throughout the year or pay a penalty for not doing so. (Chapter 13 explains this in detail.)

Freelancers should consider setting up an LLC. This not only protects you from a legal perspective, especially in fields with potential liability like consulting. It may also make sense financially. Once freelancers earn over a certain threshold, electing for the LLC to be taxed as an S Corporation for tax purposes can save money because it limits self-employment taxes. With an S Corp, you have the potential to save 15.3% of the majority of your net income, which makes it a no-brainer for freelancers who earn over a certain amount.

It usually costs a few hundred dollars to set up an LLC and maintain it each year. The exact costs depend on the state and annual requirements. For an S Corp, you will need to file an extra return as well as set up payroll for yourself. This is why it only makes sense to become an S Corp at a certain level of income.

Location-Independent Entrepreneurs

While entrepreneurs share some characteristics with freelancers, they are distinct in a few ways. Entrepreneurs are often focused on building a business and its system, whereas a freelancer is likely charging per hour or by the project for a specific service.

As they grow their business, entrepreneurs should consider incorporating. S Corps, which offer the ability to limit self-employment tax and the option to contribute more to retirement accounts, are particularly advantageous. Other entrepreneurs may benefit more from incorporating an offshore company, which would result in a 10.5% corporate tax and no self-employment taxes. The remaining earnings will be taxed at 15-20% when distributed as a dividend if the offshore company is owned by a US C Corp or in a tax treaty country. Otherwise, it will be taxed at the owner's ordinary income tax rate. In Chapter 12, we break down in more detail the benefits of different types of entities.

Hiring staff or contractors also has implications. If you hire independent US contractors and pay them $600 or more during the year, you must submit a Form 1099 for each contractor before January 31. What you need to file for employees will depend on what country they are from, where your company is incorporated, and more.

Chapter 15: Renouncing Citizenship

The number of US citizens renouncing their citizenship has increased drastically in the last decade. Complex tax filing requirements and banking hassles have accelerated this trend. However, renouncing US citizenship is not a quick fix or an easy way out of tax obligations. The process is complex and costly and can even create tax obligations. Nonetheless, with the right planning and mitigation strategies, you can minimize the implications. Still, before taking this drastic step, make sure you understand all implications of renouncing.

Tax And Other Implications Of Citizenship Renunciation

Renunciation is a decision that requires significant consideration. When giving up your US citizenship, you are surrendering all the rights associated with being an American citizen.

This includes the right to vote and your ability to visit and work in the United States. Once you renounce, you may need to apply for a visa to visit the US, unless your new country has visa free access. This can be an important factor when choosing a second passport.

This also means that you are relinquishing your right to work in the United States. As one of the strongest economies in the world, you need to be certain that you will not want or need a job in the US in the future. If you renounce and then decide to move back to the US, you will have to go through the same process and meet the same requirements as any other applicants to obtain a visa and work permit. In short, you should be confident that you will never move back to the United States.

You will also lose potential support from the US government in an emergency. Support from the US government in an emergency may seem like a far-fetched scenario. However, during the COVID-19 pandemic many US expats took advantage of humanitarian flights organized by US embassies.

Americans have many other aspects to consider before deciding to renounce. Some of these aspects will be personal, such as your financial circumstances, your long-term plans, and the expected taxation in your new country. But don't forget about the tax implications.

Renouncing your US citizenship does not mean you are free from American taxation. Even as a non-US person you can incur a US tax obligation. For example, if you have US-sourced income, such as from a rental property, you must file a tax return, even when you are not a US citizen anymore. Investing in the States as a non-citizen also has US tax implications. If a US company pays a dividend to you after you renounce, a 30% tax on the dividend is applied (unless an applicable tax treaty designates a lower withholding percentage). Chapter 6 has more information on tax treaties.

Similarly, once you are no longer a US citizen you will be subject to the rules of the Substantial Presence Test. Spending too much time in the US as a non-US person could make you a tax resident. We explain the Substantial Presence Test further in Chapter 2.

In addition, renunciation can significantly impact your estate and other gifts you plan to make. While US citizens can shield up to $11.7 million (2021) or $12.06 million (2022) from estate taxes, non-US citizens are only exempt up to $60,000. Likewise, gifts from US spouses to non-US spouses are taxed. A gift from a non-US spouse to their US spouse is taxed after only $159,000 (2021) or $164,000 (2022). On the other hand, between two US spouses, tax-free gifts are unlimited.

Fortunately for non-US persons, estate and gift taxes only apply to assets "situated" in the United States. For these reasons, it is critical to structure your estate properly.

Finally, the renunciation fees, the cost of a second citizenship, and potentially being a covered expat should also be a key factor in the decision to renounce.

Cost Of Renouncing

The renunciation fee currently is $2,350. In addition, you have to travel to a United States consulate at least once for the interview and renunciation oath. Although hefty, it is likely only a small fee compared to the cost of acquiring a second citizenship.

If you already have a second citizenship, then this may not be a concern. However, for those who do not have one, expenses can quickly add up. Citizenship by investment, offered in some countries, usually comes at a significant price tag. You can also consider citizenship through residency which is cheaper but can take many years. If eligible, you may be able to obtain a passport based on ancestry. Yet this can also take a few years and, depending on the country, it can also become expensive.

Another potential cost is catching up on back taxes. If you were not tax compliant in any of the last 5 years, then you need to file and pay back taxes. You can learn more about back taxes in Chapter 11.

Finally, Americans that are "covered expats" will need to pay an exit tax to renounce.

Covered Expats And Exit Taxes

If you renounce your US citizenship and are a "covered expat" you may have to pay an exit tax. Covered expats are US persons who meet one or more of the following categories:

- Average annual US income tax liability over the last five years is greater than $172,000 (2021)
- Net worth is equal to or greater than $2 million at the time of renunciation
- Not tax compliant during any of the last five years

Married couples must each qualify individually.

The IRS allows exceptions to the Covered Expat rules for certain dual citizens and minors. If you meet the exceptions below, the amount of your income tax liability or net worth won't matter. But you must be tax compliant and certify that by filing IRS form 8854.

- Dual citizens by birth who are still a citizen and tax-resident of the other country AND who have not been a United State resident for more than 10 of the last 15 years.
- Minors who expatriated before they are 18 ½ years old AND who have not been a United State resident for more than 10 of the last 15 years.

Covered expats, as defined above, are subject to an exit tax, when renouncing their citizenship. You could think of exit tax as the theoretical taxes incurred if you sold your entire worldwide estate and financial accounts the day before renunciation. This even applies to assets that cannot be sold, although some exceptions are made for eligible deferred compensation plans and cash in accounts. The phantom profits of these deemed sales are then taxed.

You can exclude the first $744,000 (2021, indexed annually for inflation) of deemed capital gains from the tax. Gains and losses are both included when calculating the exit tax. The taxes apply only to capital gains exceeding $744,000 (2021). If you qualify as a "covered expat" you pay tax at the highest marginal tax brackets. The exit tax is then added to the taxes owed for the year.

You should also keep in mind that your country of residence may tax profits from these same assets again if, for example, you sell the assets or receive deferred compensation.

Tax Planning Prior To Renouncing

You can minimize the tax implications of renouncing with awareness and proper planning. For example, giving away assets can help you stay below the net worth threshold of $2 million for covered expats. This can be done by moving your assets to a trust or giving assets to your spouse or next of kin.

You should also consider giving away appreciated assets to minimize the mark-to-market tax. A covered expatriate may make gifts the year before expatriation. Gifts that are made the year of expatriation are included in the exit tax. Because of this, it's important to plan out gifts several years in advance if you are planning to expatriate. American citizens can gift up to $11.7 million tax free (as of 2021) under the lifetime gifting exemption. It may be beneficial to make gifts above this amount to minimize future inheritance taxes depending on your situation. The annual exclusion amount of a gift is $15,000 in 2020 and 2021. Gifts under this amount generally don't need to be reported to the IRS. If a gift exceeds this amount, then it generally needs to report to the IRS on a gift tax return and gift taxes may be owed. However, as long as you haven't hit the lifetime gift of exclusion of $11.7 million (2021), then you shouldn't owe any taxes on the gifts. For example, if you gift your child a property worth $515,000 in 2021. This is $500,000 over the $15,000 exclusion. Because of this, you need to report the gift to the IRS. Fortunately, as long as you are still under the lifetime exclusion amount of $11.7 million (2021), you shouldn't owe any taxes on the gift. After gifting this property to your child, you now have a remaining lifetime gift exclusion of $11.2 million ($11,700,000-$500,000). There is unlimited spousal giving if your spouse is a US taxpayer.

In addition, married Americans with assets in the US may consider having only one spouse renounce. The US spouse would keep any US assets, for example, the house. The non-US spouse would take the foreign assets.

By the US spouse taking ownership of the US assets, it mitigates not only the estate tax risk. It also allows for the non-US spouse to avoid filing any US taxes or deal with withholding requirements for dividends, interest or sale of real estate (known as FIRPTA rules). It is important to note that a non-US person does not pay any capital gains tax, so in case of a lot of trading gains it would be better for the non-US spouse to hold these assets. The non-US spouse would hold all the non-US assets, therefore not needing to report foreign bank accounts, income etc. By keeping one spouse as a US person, it also allows the renouncing spouse the opportunity to get sponsored for a green card should the couple decide to return to the US.

Social Security And Retirement Payments After Renouncing

After expatriating, you are still eligible to receive social security if you previously qualified by having enough credits.

You can also still receive your 401(k) and pension, albeit both are subject to US taxes. You may have to file a 1040NR return unless taxes are automatically withheld. Military pensions however are revoked when one expatriates as the person can no longer be called into active military service as a non-citizen.

Renunciation Process

Renouncing American citizenship is not a quick event but a complex and often long process. These are the 6 steps to renounce US citizenship:

1. Obtain a second passport
2. Be up to date on your US taxes
3. Prepare expatriation paperwork
4. Book your appointment
5. Attend your renunciation appointment
6. File your final US tax return

Let's review each step in more detail.

1. Obtain A Second Passport

Even though it is your right to expatriate, the state department may deny your renunciation application if you do not have a second passport. Furthermore, if you expatriate without a second passport, you run the risk of becoming stateless if you have a visa issue in your current country of residency.

You can obtain an additional passport through investment, ancestry, or residency programs which lead to citizenship. Popular citizenship by investment programs include St. Kitts & Nevis, Malta, Montenegro, Grenada, Austria, Cyprus, Dominica, Turkey, and more. A variety of countries also offer citizenship to descendants of citizens including Luxembourg, Italy, Ireland, Poland, and more. Many countries also offer citizenship to residents though this is not usually an option until after several years of residency.

Remember to bring the second passport to your renunciation appointment.

2. Be Up To Date On Your US Taxes

In order to expatriate and not automatically be considered a covered expat, you need to be up to date on filing the last 5 years of tax returns. If you haven't filed your US taxes, visit Chapter 11.

3. Prepare Expatriation Paperwork

You will need to fill out the form called "Request for Determination of Possible Loss of US Citizenship," also known as form DS-4079, and attach supporting documents, including a birth certificate or certificate of naturalization from the country of your second passport.

Be aware that the reason for renunciation cannot be taxes. You need to have a valid reason. For example, a stronger connection to another country, you no longer live in the United States and will not return, or an injustice experienced as an American.

4. Book Your Appointment

Ideally, book your appointment at the embassy or consulate in the country or city where you plan to live once you renounce your passport. However, if you are not able to, you can also use a consulate in another country or city.

You may be able to save time by going to a neighboring country to renounce as some of the more common countries have waiting lists of over a year (UK, Canada, Singapore, etc.). It makes sense to shop around and research the consulates. Besides wait times for appointments, there are process inconsistencies. Some require at least two visits, others let you complete it in one day.

5. Attend Your Renunciation Appointment

Make sure you bring the following to your renunciation appointment:

- US passport
- Second passport
- Birth certificate
- Certificate of naturalization associated with the second passport

At the end of your appointment, you will receive a Certificate of Loss of Nationality (CLN).

6. File Your Final US Tax Return

Your final tax return as an American citizen will be from January 1 through the day that you expatriate. From the day you renounce you are no longer a taxable person to the IRS. If your renunciation date is any day other than December 31, you will need to file a "dual status return" which includes filing both a Form 1040 and 1040NR (if applicable). You should always file both of them, even if the 1040NR is blank.

You will need to file Form 8854 which declares whether you are a covered expatriate or not and will calculate your exit tax, if applicable. Failure to file this form means you are still liable for US income tax indefinitely – even if you have completed renunciation for immigration purposes.

If you had foreign accounts already in existence before expatriation, you will also need to file FinCEN Form 114 also known as the FBAR. Keep in mind that if you still have income in the US, including pensions or rental properties, you must still file annual tax returns.

The timeframe to renounce citizenship varies depending on several factors including how long it takes you to obtain a second passport, whether you are caught up on your US taxes, and how busy the embassy you book your appointment at is. Some embassies process a high-volume of renunciations and may have a waitlist. Consider inquiring at several embassies to find one with a short wait time.

Penalties For Not Filing The Expatriation Form

You must file your IRS Form 8854 when you expatriate. If you do not, you could be subject to a significant fine from the IRS. As of 2021, the fine for failure to submit this form is $10,000. The IRS takes this issue seriously and will send notices to expatriates who have not complied. They apply the penalty of $10,000 as appropriate. In some specific situations, the new Relief Procedures for Certain Former Citizens may eliminate the taxes, interest, penalties and exit taxes incurred when relinquishing citizenship.

Renunciation Relief For Accidental Americans

Accidental Americans who acquired US citizenship through birth but never lived there often have a rude awakening when they find out that they were supposed to file US tax returns every year. Fortunately, the IRS currently offers relief through the Relief Procedures for Certain Former Citizens. The relief is only available for Americans who meet strict requirements. If accidental Americans qualify under these rules, they must still submit their prior five years of tax returns before renouncing. But they won't be liable to pay any tax or penalties. Keep in mind that this is difficult to qualify for.

Applicants must meet all of the following criteria:

1. Net worth of less than $2 million at the time of renunciation or at the time of entering the program

2. Filed a US tax return and applicable reporting forms for the year you renounce and the five previous years, plus Form 8854 for the renunciation year
3. Had an aggregate federal income tax liability of less than $25,000 or less during the year you renounce and the five previous years (excluding interest or penalties)
4. Any previous failure to file taxes or report was non-willful

As with any IRS relief program, this may end in the future. If it applies to you, you should use it while it is available.

Chapter 16: Filing Your Expat Tax Return

Why not save some money and do it yourself or stick with the tax preparer you had in the US? The biggest issue is that neither are experts in taxes for Americans abroad. This leaves taxpayers vulnerable to errors, overpayments, and lost opportunities to claim valuable tax benefits.

DIY Software

Taxes for Americans overseas are not as simple as going through a TurboTax or TaxAct questionnaire. These programs are made for the typical US taxpayer, not for expats facing complex international issues. To properly file taxes as an American abroad, you must dive deep into tax forms and IRS publications and spend hours trying to get it right. Even then, there will always be that uncertainty.

Once we saw that a commonly used self-tax preparation software missed a $20,000 tax loss carryover on a rental property that the taxpayer had sold. If this software had realized the rental loss carryovers, the taxpayer could have claimed a $20,000 tax loss on his schedule E. Without this, his tax bill was significantly higher than it should have been. Filing this incorrect return wasn't cheap either. He paid around $120 for his federal and state return, wasted three hours working in front of the computer, and, in the end, the software missed a massive tax savings opportunity. This was a simple domestic-based tax issue. We've seen countless problems with the expat-related parts of the return.

US-Based CPA

The tax accountant who did your taxes when you were living in the US is probably awesome. However, he or she likely doesn't have experience with the unique aspects of taxes for US persons overseas. A US-based CPA with over 30 years of experience may only see one expat related return every five years or so. When working with a US

CPA you could miss out on uncommon deductions or exclusions that a firm specializing in tax for Americans overseas would spot immediately.

Once we saw a situation where someone was living in Malta, let's call him Blake, and had only spent 50 days working in the US. At the end of the year, his employer issued him a W-2. Blake's previous accountant didn't realize that you must source even a W-2 between the US and the host country. The accountant incorrectly put in the return that all of Blake's income that year was US-sourced. When we reviewed the return, we were able to determine that he was eligible for the Foreign Earned Income Exclusion. We amended the return and allocated about $70,000 as sourced in Malta and excluded it with the FEIE. He received a refund of over $10,000 from the IRS.

Expat Tax Experts

Expat tax experts have experience with the myriad of tax situations that Americans abroad face. We can help you where US-based CPAs can't. At Online Taxman, we have filed thousands of US expat tax returns for American employees, contractors, business owners, digital nomads, and retirees, all over the world.

How To Choose An Accountant

When you do a Google search for the best expat tax service or similar search terms, you probably first see a couple of ads, maybe even one of ours. We could just say, you can stop your search because you found the best, us. But of course, we are a little biased. So how do you decide whom to trust with your tax and financial information? How to select from the tax services marketed online and recommendations from friends? After all, when spending money on getting your taxes done, you want the peace of mind that they are done correctly, and tax savings are optimized.

Here we give you a list of questions you should ask a CPA or expatriate tax services firm when looking for a tax accountant.

1. What Is Your Experience With Expat Tax?

This seems like a no-brainer, but we see US taxpayers lose out on tax savings opportunities because their US-based CPA didn't know about them. Even the best CPA for US domestic tax returns may not be familiar with Form 2555, Form 1116, FBAR, Form 8938, Form 5471, Dual Resident Returns, the Foreign Housing Exclusion or Deduction, etc. Don't worry if you don't know these forms or terms, but your CPA should know them in their sleep. You may want to ask how many Americans overseas he or she has worked with in the last few years.

When working with a tax accounting firm rather than an individual CPA, you should also ask about the experience of the person who will actually prepare your return and if there is anyone else reviewing it.

2. Can I Ask You Tax Questions Throughout The Year?

As a US person living outside of the US, we are often faced with big changes in our lives that may affect our tax situation – marriage to a foreign spouse, foreign pensions or investment opportunities, moving stateside or to another country. Will you be able to call up your CPA to obtain tax guidance throughout the year? Or would you have to pay extra for that service? As an FYI, we include this service with the fixed fee of working with us on your annual tax return preparation.

3. What If You Make A Mistake On My Return? Are You Insured?

Mistakes shouldn't happen, but we are all human. A good accountant carries Errors & Omissions insurance to cover those issues. But many others limit their maximum liability to the fee you paid for their service. Again, please read the fine print. This is often covered in the Terms of Service or Terms of Engagement or a similarly titled document. Or ask during the consultation, which might be easier.

4. What If The IRS Has Questions About My Return? Will You Help?

A good accountant should stand a hundred percent behind the return he prepared. He or she should handle all questions from the IRS about the return on your behalf without extra charge.

Sometimes the IRS might want a full audit of your books, which would be your responsibility to show receipts. However, a CPA should be available to guide you, not run away from your problems.

We at Online Taxman will address all IRS inquiries with a written correspondence when applicable, which is also included in our service fee.

5. What Is Your Process?

Expats are on the move. Coming to an office or depending on US business hours is not feasible for many. Tax documents should only be transmitted via a secure encrypted online portal. A CPA should never send or request tax documents attached to an email.

The tax accounting firm should explain the overall process to you. You should also get your accountant's contact information, usually an email address or a phone or Skype number, not just the general office number.

Additional Considerations For Freelancers And Small Business Owners To Find The Best Tax Accountant

If you plan to incorporate, make sure your CPA asks you about your income levels, location, business/fundraising goals, before recommending a course of action, such as opening an LLC, switching from LLC to S Corp, or opening a foreign company. If you already have a business, ask your tax accountant about the tax law changes and any steps you can take to tax-optimize your business.

Chapter 17: Tax Due Dates And Recordkeeping

Expat Tax Calendar

The US tax deadline for expats to file an individual tax return is different than for Americans at home. US persons residing abroad get an automatic 2-month filing extension for individual returns. Instead of having an April 15 deadline, expats have until June 15 to file and pay any tax due. Keep in mind that if you owe tax, interest still starts accruing from April 15, but you will not be otherwise penalized until after June 15.

Americans overseas are eligible for this extension starting April 15 of the year after the tax year that they are filing for. In other words, if you move abroad in 2021, then you are eligible for this extension in 2022 when you are filing taxes for 2021.

If you need more time to file, you can request an extension to October 15. This can be helpful if you need more time to qualify for the FEIE (more on this in Chapter 3) or if you live in a country where taxes are filed later in the year, such as Hong Kong, Germany, Colombia, Australia, France, and the UK. An extension to October 15 is requested on Form 4868. In some cases, expats can request an extension to December 15 or even January 30. However, to avoid late payment penalties, any tax due must be paid by the June 15 deadline.

Below is a calendar that lists important due dates for US expats and entrepreneurs abroad by month.

January 15

- Fourth installment of quarterly estimated taxes for the previous calendar year due

January 31

- Submit Form 1099 for contractors before January 31

February 1

- Last day to file and pay all quarterly estimated taxes without penalties (only applicable if the last quarterly installment wasn't paid on January 15)

March 15

- S-Corp tax return initial due date
- Multi-member LLC tax return initial due date
- Trust returns due for US individuals with US or foreign trusts initial due date

April 15

- Individual tax return due if residing in the US (include Form 8938, Statement of Specified Foreign Financial Assets, if applicable)
- Payment of tax due (interest starts accruing on unpaid taxes after April 15, even for expats).
- Initial FBAR deadline
- C-Corporation tax return initial due date
- First installment of quarterly estimated taxes due for the current calendar year

June 15

- Individual tax return due if residing outside the US
- Second installment of quarterly estimated taxes due

September 15

- Extended filing deadline for S-Corporations (extension must be requested)
- Extended filing deadline for multi-member LLCs (extension must be requested)
- Extended filing deadline for US trusts or foreign trusts owned US individuals (extension must be requested)
- Third installment of quarterly estimated taxes due

October 15

- Extended filing deadline for individual US tax returns (extension must be requested)
- Extended filing deadline for C-Corporations (extension must be requested)

Be sure to confirm the deadlines that apply to you every year. When a deadline falls on a weekend or holiday, the date changes. For example, if in a given year, June 15 falls on a Saturday, then the deadline moves to the following Monday, June 17. In exceptional circumstances, as we have seen during the coronavirus pandemic, the government can extend tax deadlines.

Tax And Other Records You Should Keep

Most of us dread recording keeping but it makes a huge difference when tax season arrives. Few things are worse than digging through paperwork, receipts, and emails at the last minute. If you don't already have a system for organizing important documents and information, think about developing one. Digital copies of your records are usually sufficient. Be sure to name the files clearly, including the document name and the year. Not only will this help you stay organized, but it will also help your accountant prepare your return as efficiently as possible. Storing a second copy of these records on a drive or in a cloud service is also a good practice.

Keep in mind that each person's tax situation is different and more or fewer records may be needed. Nonetheless, the below list is a good place to start.

In general, taxpayers should keep anything that supports their income, deductions, or credits. This is especially important for US persons who may be excluding or deducting a large part of their income. If you don't have the right records you could miss out on a refund or credit.

Regardless of how you store your tax records, you should keep them for at least three years. The IRS can audit returns for up to three years after they are submitted. When a taxpayer fails to report 25% or more of their income, the IRS has up to six years from the filing date to initiate an audit.

Here are the most common tax records expat need to keep:

Prior Year Tax Returns

The last 2-3 years of tax returns are a good starting point to review what you might need for the current filing. If you work with an accountant, they should review these to make sure items such as the Foreign Tax Credit are carried over. Tax returns from previous years contain the information needed to carry over unused credits correctly.

Keep prior state and local tax records as well. If you paid and state or local taxes, you need records for the amount you paid.

Foreign Tax Records

If you paid taxes in a foreign country, you may be eligible for a foreign tax credit. You need records that show the amount and type of foreign tax paid. Foreign tax records justify any foreign tax credits claimed on your US tax return. Most Americans who are residents of a foreign country will have a foreign tax return. Some expats may also file city, state, or provincial tax returns in foreign countries.

Travel Dates

If you plan to claim the Foreign Earned Income Exclusion or the Foreign Tax Credit, you need to keep detailed records of your travel dates in and out of the US. To track travel dates, consider keeping a spreadsheet that includes arrival and departure dates in the US. This information will be included in your tax return when claiming the FEIE. When claiming the Foreign Tax Credit on earned income, you need a record of how many days you worked in the US because you cannot use the credit on income earned in the United States. We also recommend saving PDFs of boarding passes or ticket purchase confirmations. We recommend that you save old passports for reference or at least scan all pages into a PDF before discarding.

Records of your travel dates are important regardless of whether you use the Physical Presence Test or the Bona Fide Residence Test. Losing or not collecting these records can cause significant issues. Because they aren't needed for the tax filing, many taxpayers forget them. But if there is an IRS audit, these records are crucial.

Proof Of Bona Fide Residence

To claim bona fide residence in a foreign country, you need to show that you are actually a resident there. The type of records vary depending on the situation but generally speaking, visa documents, local ID card, bank statements, driver's license, health insurance card, and any other documentation showing local ties. You won't need those records for the tax filing but in case of an audit.

Income Records

Whether your income is from wages or salary, self-employment income, investments, dividends, sale of property or assets, you should save the records or statements that show the income.

For taxpayers employed with a US company, income is reported on a W-2 form. Unless abroad on an assignment with a US company, foreign employers do not provide W-2s. In this case, you can use a year-end statement, salary statement, or other documents that show income and tax withheld, if any.

Independent contractors should have received a 1099 form if the income from one contract exceeded $600. However, non-US clients likely will not provide you with a 1099 or similar form. You must still report all income and can use any record, bank statement or other statements.

Self-employed taxpayers should prepare a statement that shows business income and expenses. This can be a simple Excel spreadsheet. These records are only needed to prepare the return and in the case of an IRS audit.

It is also important to be able to document your expenses via receipts if you get audited. Having a picture or a scan of a receipt (or using an app such as Expensify) if acceptable.

If you are paying US contractors, you should have a W-9 for your records and provide a Form 1099 to them. If they are foreign contractors, you should have a W-8BEN form for your records. Ideally, you should be getting this documentation during the hiring process, so you don't need to chase them down later.

Other income can include rental income, social security or pension benefits, annuities, other retirement income such as IRA distributions, unemployment benefits, income from gambling, K1s from partnerships and S Corps, royalties, and more. Keep records for all types of income.

Investment Income Records

This includes records for interest, dividends, sales of bonds or stocks, foreign investments, securities, cryptocurrency, and more.

US banks and financial institutions usually issue a 1099 form for interest income, dividend income, proceeds from the sale of bonds or stocks, and income from foreign investments. You can also use a year-end statement from your bank. These records can be difficult to collect from foreign banks because they may not issue a year-end statement. When that happens, bank statements might work instead.

If you bought and/or sold stock or other securities, your broker should send you a statement, usually a 1099 form. If the statement does not contain information about the cost basis you would need to provide that yourself. If you sold securities, you will also need the date the security was acquired. This information is the same for cryptocurrency investments, you will need cost basis (purchase price/quantity, purchase date) and the sale info (sale proceeds, sale dates) which may be harder to track, since there is no formal reporting such as a 1099 form. Hence, self-reporting and recordkeeping are required.

Similarly, you would need this information for any foreign investments you own. Foreign financial institutions may not issue a 1099 or similar forms, so the reporting burden is on you.

Business Income

When owning a business, you will need records of the business income and expenses as you are responsible for reporting that income. The structure of the business (sole proprietor, LLC, S Corp, or Foreign Corp) will determine which form you would need to fill out for the tax return (Schedule C vs. 1120S vs. 5471). Regardless of the form, you will need to produce a profit/loss statement and potentially a balance sheet summary of the assets, liabilities, and equity.

If you are a partial owner of a US partnership or S Corp, you should expect a K-1, which summarizes your allocated portion of income or loss to be reported on your tax return.

An owner of a foreign company or C Corp should self-report any dividends, salaries, or other income received.

Real Estate Related Documents

If you own real property you may need the following tax records for your tax return:

- Rental income and expenses – a property management company may provide you with a statement or you will need to keep a profit/loss statement for the property.
- Mortgage interest – reported on form 1098 in the US, foreign mortgage interest information is generally provided by foreign banks.
- Purchase or sale of real property
- Cost basis of improvements made to the property

Foreign Housing Expenses

As an American abroad, you may be able to exclude or deduct foreign housing expenses. For that, you need records of your housing expenses including rent, utilities, repairs, parking, furniture rental, etc. This is generally only needed in the case of an audit to justify the use of the Foreign Housing Exclusion or Deduction.

These same documents may also be useful for the Bona Fide Residence Test.

Value Of Foreign Bank Accounts

These records are needed for filing the FBAR. Some banks may issue an end-of-year statement. If not, keep your bank statements. You must have records of the highest balance of each account during the year.

Importantly, if you bank online, make sure that you download the bank statements. Do not rely on the bank to always have them online. One team member at Online Taxman once had issues getting statements from her online bank abroad. The bank only kept statements online from the last three months. Any statements older than three months old had to be requested in person at a bank branch for $7 per statement or via phone for $12 per statement. Moreover, if requested at the branch the statements could only be printed (not emailed) and you had to pay in cash.

Foreign Assets

Expats also often need to keep records of their foreign bank accounts and foreign financial assets such as foreign mutual funds, pensions, and life insurance schemes.

These assets are reported on Form 8938. Fortunately, the threshold for expats to file is relatively high.

Other Records

As always, be sure to discuss the specifics of your situation with your accountant. You may need additional records depending on your specific tax situation. Some examples to consider are payments made to a foreign childcare provider (for the Child Care Tax Credit).

———————————

Printed in Great Britain
by Amazon

38513161R00079